Russell D. Longcore

INSURANCE CLAIM SECRETS

REVEALED!

TAKE CONTROL OF YOUR INSURANCE CLAIMS !
ADD HUNDREDS OR THOUSANDS MORE DOLLARS TO YOUR CLAIM SETTLEMENT!

D1500540

www.trafford.com

North America & international
toll-free: 1 888 232 4444 (USA & Canada)
phone: 250 383 6864 ♦ fax: 250 383 6804
email: info@trafford.com

The United Kingdom & Europe
phone: +44 (0)1865 487 395 ♦ local rate: 0845 230 9601
facsimile: +44 (0)1865 481 507 ♦ email: info.uk@trafford.com

10 9

Russell D. Longcore has been nominated by the Georgia Writers Association for the 2008 Georgia Author of the Year Award! The Georgia Writers Association is affiliated with the Department of Humanities at Kennesaw State University, and is funded by the Georgia General Assembly and the National Endowment for the Arts. This is the 44th annual awards ceremony, and is the most prestigious writing award in the State of Georgia.

This book is Russell's first book! The book is written about insurance claims...not exactly an exciting subject. So, can you imagine how compelling and important this book must be for Russell to receive such a prestigious nomination for an award?

* * * *

On October 20, 2008, Russell D. Longcore was notified that this book was a Finalist in the USA Book News Best Book Awards 2008! The book was listed in the category Personal Finance. You could not do better for your personal finances than to buy and read this book!

* * * *

William "Chip" Merlin is a nationally-known attorney who goes beyond the fine print. His Tampa, Florida law firm solely represents the rights of residential and commercial policyholders.

Here is his stunning quote: "Insurance is one of the most important financial products any person or business can purchase. The sad reality of the insurance industry's broken promises is made transparent through the astonishing revelations by Russell Longcore in this book."

* * * *

"Thanks for writing your book. It explains things so the rest of us can understand."

Dawn A., Houston, TX

* * * *

"I was really glad when I came across your book. I wish we had come across it sooner. Thank you for writing a book and making yourself available for questions."

Marie R., Warren, NJ

* * * *

"Hey Russ,

Great book! I am sure I will give your books away as gifts too..."

Andy S., Westminster, MA

"I heard the DJ on the local radio station talking about Russell's book, so I immediately downloaded it when I got to work. It has been a great help to me. Not only does it talk about vehicle accidents but property damage and more, as well. I would recommend anyone dealing with an insurance company to buy this book. Well worth the knowledge you gain to determine if the insurance company is treating you fairly. Knowledge is power when dealing with insurance companies."

Lisa W., Winston, GA

* * * *

"Russell D. Longcore deals with this head-on, and in terms that you and I can easily understand. His honest, direct, straight-forward approach is excellent.

It's not a question of "if" you're going to need to know and understand the facts about which Longcore writes in this book - but "when." Longcore addresses those things which the insurance industry would just as soon you never knew, and certainly won't tell you, until after-the-fact. Based on personal experience, I hope it's not too late for you.

If you're considering the purchase of a new policy, or are about to renew a policy - regardless of the type - READ THIS BOOK FIRST.

INSURANCE CLAIM SECRETS REVEALED! is a book deserving of a FIVE STAR rating, because it will guide you in your thought process, and protect you in ways that you've never suspected, nor imagined. Pass it up at your own peril."

Sanders H., Atlanta, GA

* * * *

"At the end of Feb. 2008 a tornado went through our neighborhood. Fortunately the damage we sustained was inconvenient damage. We had several trees down, one unfortunately hit the back of our car, and lots of debris, and the top of our neighbor's pine tree was dropped onto our roof. We called our insurance agent to report and started the clean-up. The weekend after the storm I was listening to the radio and heard Russell Longcore being interview by Elyse Glink. I was so impressed, I immediately got online to his website and bought the E-book. It downloaded right away and I started to read. Fortunately our house is now back together and we are only out of pocket the amount of our deductible. There is so much information in this book and it's easy to read and understand. No one should be without it."

Dee K, Atlanta, GA

Disclaimer

The information in this book is general in nature and does not take into account each and every situation that could possibly arise. You must thoroughly review your own insurance policy to determine your rights and responsibilities, and the rights and responsibilities of the insurance company. The information provided herein is intended to be current and accurate. However, such information may not be sufficient to deal with your individual situation.

Trafford Publishing, the author, contributors or distributors do not warrant, guarantee or represent in any manner that the information presented herein is suitable for you. No portion of this book is intended to provide you with legal advice regarding your individual policy or claim. The information herein is meant to assist and guide you, and should not be relied upon as a substitute for independent research, tax and legal advice. Before acting on our advice, we recommend that you seek legal counsel from your attorney.

The laws governing each state will not only vary, but are continuously subject to change. We strongly urge you to seek legal advice before taking any action.

Cover art beautifully done by Daniel Wright.

This book is dedicated to my Redhead, Julia Ann.

You are the great love of my life.

Table of Contents

INTRODUCTION

There's a little song that says, "Love makes the world go around." I hate to be the one to tell you this…but that's not true.

There's also a song in the musical "Cabaret", that says, "Money makes the world go around." That's a little closer to reality, but still not all the way true.

Insurance makes the world go around.

Nearly everything that we touch, and nearly everything that touches us, is insured. Without insurance, most of the everyday products and services we just accept as normal could only be purchased by the wealthy. Without insurance, businesses could not protect themselves from liability lawsuits. There would not be thousands of ships that carry cargo between nations, as investors in the ships and the cargo could not be sure they wouldn't be financially wiped out if their ships sank on the high seas.

If it weren't for insurance, very few people would ever get a home mortgage or an automobile loan. Think about it….what bank would lend YOU money for a house when their collateral might burn to the ground? Same for a car…what bank would lend money when the car could be destroyed in an accident?

Closer to home, people who were found to be negligent in a

court of law would be financially wiped out making restitution to their victims. People would be reluctant to even drive their car to the market for fear of getting in an accident that was their fault.

Our world would be very different, and our capitalist system of economics would be radically different without insurance. Just think of how the world economics worked just 400 years ago in the days before insurance was invented.

That's what our world would be like today without insurance.

A significant portion of every adult's income is spent for insurance. We insure our health, our lives, our vehicles, our businesses, our homes and our toys.

Have you ever heard the term "insurance poor?" That's the feeling one gets when he sees a large portion of his disposable income paid out in insurance premiums. It usually also means that the person doesn't think that they're getting their money's worth. I say that because people don't usually complain about the price of something if they perceive that the value is worth the price. I've heard LOTS of people say that they're "insurance poor," and I know how they feel.

Yet, for all of the money that consumers spend on insurance, hardly anyone understands how it works. Fewer still ever read the policies that they buy. That lack of understanding leaves the consumer very vulnerable, and likely to receive far less money in any insurance settlement than the amount that they are entitled to collect.

I'll tell you a story about my own recent auto accident in Chapter Twenty Three, and how much money I could have lost if I had not been prepared. There's also a story in Chapter One about my homeowner's claim, and the thousands of dollars I collected that would not normally have been paid out.

But first, let me tell you a little bit about me.

I've been around the insurance business since 1973. In late 1972, my wife and I bought our first house for $21,500.00. Three little bedrooms, one bath, 1008 square feet on a half-acre lot. It wasn't much, but it was ours.   Naturally, we bought a homeowners insurance policy just before closing…the bank required it. In January of 1973, Gary Sherman, the Farm Bureau Insurance agent who sold the policy came to the house one evening to deliver the policy, and try to sell us auto and life insurance. I don't remember if he was successful that night in selling us more insurance, but he asked me if I'd be interested in becoming an insurance agent.

I was nineteen years old, working as a laborer in my father's construction company, in January in Michigan. I wasn't real excited about working outdoors, and didn't see much future in it. This guy was offering me inside work…wearing a coat and tie.

What do you _think_ I said?

YES!!!

By the end of April, I had passed my state licensing exams, and gotten my agent licenses. I was on my way as a Farm Bureau Insurance agent. I was the youngest agent that the company had ever hired in their history. Soon after that, Gary and his manager Jim Wood3 moved down the street and started an independent agency. I joined them.

After five years, I went back into the family construction business, and eventually became Vice President of the three construction companies we owned. I always kept my licenses active, and sold various types of insurance on a part-time basis.

In 1986, I sold my portion of the construction companies back to my Dad, and went back into insurance sales full-time. I sold term life insurance and investment securities, and did pretty well.

In 1992, we moved from West Michigan to Atlanta, Georgia. Shortly after arriving here in Atlanta, Hurricane Andrew devastated

South Florida and Louisiana. The insurance companies were completely overloaded with claims, as were the independent claims adjusting companies that served those insurance companies. In those instances, insurance companies and adjusting companies rely heavily on temporary adjusters..."storm troopers," as they are called. The companies look for people with either insurance experience or construction experience.

I had both.

A national independent adjusting company hired me immediately, and in a few days I was in Miami.

What an amazing experience catastrophe adjusting (CAT duty) was!! I remember, on my first day, standing on the roof of a one story house in Kendall, Florida, measuring and making a diagram of what was left of the roof. I looked up, and as far as the eye could see in every direction were roofs with blue tarps on them.

Even right then, I knew I would love claims adjusting.

I could hardly believe that someone was going to pay me a lot of money to look at damages and write estimates. I'd been writing estimates for years. I thought I'd died and gone to heaven.

(I hope that you have work that you love. Most of the people that I know don't like what they do for a living.)

Once the CAT duty was over, I came back to Atlanta, and soon I'd found a full-time job with an independent adjusting company. I've been a claims adjuster ever since.

There's a position in the claims adjusting field that's called a "General Adjuster," or GA. It's kind of like being a General in the military. The GA position is as high as an adjuster can go. To qualify, you have to take a lot of insurance coursework, have a peer review of your claims handling work, and have a depth of experience.

It normally takes an adjuster at least ten to fifteen years to attain this position. I made it in four years. Now, I'm an Executive General Adjuster. That means I handle the most complicated and huge losses, and supervise the work of other adjusters.

I've had some of the best training in claims that a fellow could possibly get. The companies I worked for kept sending me to various schools, each one more advanced than the last. I also did a lot of study through trade institutes. That helped me rocket forward in the claims business.

For a couple of years, I even did work for an insurance company as Home Office General Adjuster and property Claims Examiner. I got an insider's look at how claims are processed in an insurance company claims department. Boy, did my eyes get opened by that experience! It's one thing to investigate a claim as an adjuster, and then send a report to a claims examiner at the insurance company. It's a whole different experience to be the claims examiner, making the decisions on what is covered and what is not covered...what claims get paid, how much gets paid, and what claims get denied.

One of the most important things that I learned as a Claims Examiner was that people were usually not very impressed with the adjuster that handled their claim. The best adjusters are detail oriented, curious and self-motivated. Unfortunately, many adjusters are not thorough, seldom curious, and somewhat lazy. Most of the reports I received were mediocre in quality. There were a notable few adjusters who did a superb job.

I think I've adjusted just about every kind of claim you could think of...homeowners, automobile, worker's compensation, ocean cargo, trucking, inland marine, jeweler's block, liability, business income, commercial property...and loved every minute of it. The money hasn't been bad, either.

An Executive General Adjuster bills his hourly time at $175.00. That's my hourly rate.

Friends, I'm haven't told you all of this history to brag. I'd just like you to know that I know what I'm talking about in the insurance sales and the insurance claims businesses.

Just like you, I've been an insurance consumer all of my adult life…even earlier, as a teenager with my '59 Jeep. But, unlike most of you, I've had the chance to experience both sides of the insurance world…. as a consumer, then as an agent and adjuster.

That's why I am so excited about writing this book!

Here's exactly why I wrote this book. Most of the people for whom I've adjusted claims had never had a property or casualty insurance claim before. (We're not dealing with health, life or worker's compensation insurance in this book. We can get to those topics in my monthly newsletters. If you're reading this book as a eBook, click here if you'd like a free subscription. Or if you're reading the paperback book, look on the back cover for my website address. Please register for the free newsletter there.). Most of those same people had NEVER read their policy, even after filing the claim. They had no idea what the claims process was, and they relied on me…the adjuster…to walk them through the process.

It is for you, and people just like you that I write this book. Many times, people who have had a loss are on the raw edge of emotion. Isn't is natural to be fearful in a situation where you don't feel you're in control…where you don't know what will happen next, and you're scared you'll be "ripped off?" Most everyone has heard a story from a relative or friend about an insurance claim that went badly.

People like that need solid advice and a strategy on what to do to get their claim paid.

They need to understand the claims process completely so that they are not at the mercy of the insurance company, the claims adjuster and the claims examiner.

They need to be paid every dollar that they are entitled to collect.

They need to have peace of mind knowing that their claim was handled correctly.

Insurance companies rely upon the ignorance of their own policyholders. So do many claims adjusters. An uninformed policyholder will rarely argue with an adjuster, <u>because they don't know what they don't know</u>.

Let me repeat that phrase so you can think about it long and hard.

<u>MOST POLICYHOLDERS OR CLAIMANTS DON'T KNOW WHAT THEY DON'T KNOW.</u>

They don't know what is in their insurance policy, and they don't know the claims process, and that lack of knowledge can cost them thousands in settlement dollars and <u>all</u> of their peace of mind.

Everything that you must do to file a claim is in your insurance policy. WHAT'S MISSING IS HOW TO DO IT.

Think of it this way: I hand you a blueprint for a small house, and tell you, "Build this house over there on that lot." I've told you WHAT to do...I've even given you a document that tells you what must be done. WHAT'S MISSING IS HOW TO TAKE THAT BLUEPRINT AND BUILD THE HOUSE.

Do you know how to pour concrete or lay cement blocks?

Do you know how to install shingles?

Do you know how to install electrical wiring?

You may build a house, but it probably won't look anything like what's on that blueprint.

If you've never built a house before, you won't know what to do first...or next...or last.

House building takes experience. Or it takes very detailed instructions on how to build a house…step by step with no steps left out.

If you have NO EXPERIENCE in house building, then you must either rely on someone who does have that experience, or you must follow step-by-step instructions…or some combination of both.

<u>That principle is exactly the same in filing an insurance claim of any type</u>. It doesn't matter if you're in the United States, or Canada, or Brazil, or Panama, or Germany, or France, or Egypt, or South Africa, or China, or India.

It doesn't matter if your claim is a Homeowner, or Auto, or Commercial Property, or Liability, or whatever kind you may have. If you have NO experience in filing a claim successfully, and getting every dollar you're entitled to collect, then you must rely on either someone who does have that experience, or you must follow the step-by-step instructions IN THIS BOOK…or some combination of both.

Insurance companies can increase their profits on your lack of knowledge. (To read about other ways insurance companies increase their profits at your expense, read Chapter Two.)

I believe that what you don't know <u>can</u> hurt you…it could even change the course of your life for the rest of your life. I believe that your lack of knowledge about the claims process could change the destiny of your children's lives and generations into the future.

For example, consider a family who owns a home. The house burns to the ground, and everything they own burns with it. The family didn't know that they had to keep their home insured to value, and did not have enough coverage. So the insurance company hits them with a co-insurance penalty that reduces their settlement by a big percentage. (This topic is explored in Chapter Twenty One.) The family did not do a good job of taking inventory of their contents, because now they are forced to do it from memory, as the contents are now ashes. The contents are not insured for replacement cost, and the contents portion of the policy is settled for Actual Cash Value, or depreciated dollars. Their choice is to either take money out of savings, children's college funds or their retirement savings to pay the difference. Another choice…if they don't have any savings, is to simply rebuild or buy a smaller house and replace their belongings with a lot less belongings. That is, after paying off the mortgage of the house that burned.

Or, they could just rent a house forever.

Mom and Dad have their lives permanently altered for the rest of their lives. Because of the fire, there's no money for college, and the children don't go to college.

Everybody in that story suffered because Mom and Dad were not prepared. Even the grandchildren yet unborn will have their lives affected because their parents did not get a college degree, and that affected their parents' ability to earn a higher income.

You see? One loss, not properly handled, can affect your destiny and your children's destiny, and generations to come. You may accuse me of melodrama, but this stuff happens regularly.

Read this book, and make sure it doesn't happen to you.

Remember the scene in the movie, "The Wizard of Oz," where Dorothy and her friends are standing before the Wizard? He's making big noises, and shooting off fire, and scaring them silly. Just then, Toto tugs on a curtain off to one side, and reveals a rotund little man behind that curtain throwing switches and moving levers. At this point in the story, Oz thunders, "PAY NO ATTENTION TO THAT MAN BEHIND THE CURTAIN!!!"

The insurance claims process is a lot like that. The companies don't want their policyholders to question the claims procedure, or figure out that it can work very differently from the way that it looks. Insurance companies and claims adjusters want policyholders and claimants to be compliant and trusting. That decreases the size of the settlements, and increases the profits of the insurance companies.

I'm going to be your "Toto." In this book, and at my website, I'm going to pull back the curtain and show you how things really work. I'll show you how you can take control of your insurance claims and your policies, and add hundreds...even many thousands of dollars...to your insurance claim settlements. These are dollars that you are ALREADY entitled to collect from your policy.

In addition to the "how-to" parts of the book, I'm going to include some stories of claims I've actually handled over the years. They're stranger than fiction...some are kind of gruesome...and all true.

Dorothy had a little dog and three friends that helped her get to the Land of Oz. That was her team. Let's stop for a minute and think about teams.

I started playing baseball on the Pee Wee League team in Kent City, Michigan, in the summer of 1962. I was 8 years old. I was always a second string first baseman, because my cousin Thomas was better than me at everything...hitting, running, fielding. All of the kids on that team were from that little village of about 600 people in West Michigan, and we had been playing together since kindergarten.

We won the league championship that year...and the same boys kept playing together as we got older. Our coaches were Don Kik and Pete Imkamp, and they administered discipline and love in equal doses to a bunch of small town boys.

We won every championship every summer until I was 14...Pee Wee League, Little League, Pony League, Junior Varsity. The summer I turned 14, we moved to a bigger town (a whopping 2,500 people) where my Dad had a construction business. As a sophomore in the spring of 1969, I finally became a starting first baseman. I played on the Junior Varsity at school, and that team won the conference championship.

I never knew what it was like to play on a baseball team that was not the champion. But remember, I wasn't the star on any of those teams. I was an average player on a championship team.

But I still got to share in the glory…just like a star.

Have you ever been on a sports team? Did you play Little League baseball, or Youth Soccer, or football, or basketball? If you did, you know how important it is to have great players on your team.

You also probably remember how painful it was when your team lost.

Friends, the stakes are way too high when it comes to handling an insurance claim.

<u>You cannot afford to have your team lose now.</u>

When it comes to your insurance coverage…no matter what kind of insurance…you need to have a team. But…

WHO DO YOU HAVE ON YOUR TEAM?

The insurance company has well trained adjusters who are experts in the claims process.

ANYONE LIKE THAT ON YOUR TEAM?

The insurance company has well trained claims examiners who are experts on reading and interpreting YOUR insurance contract.

ANYONE LIKE THAT ON YOUR TEAM?

The insurance company has staff attorneys that can answer their questions if a legal issue comes up in your claim. The company will hire the best trial lawyers money can buy to defend the insurance company in court if your claim goes to trial.

ANYONE LIKE THAT ON YOUR TEAM?

The insurance company has Training and Compliance experts to make sure that the claim is handled correctly, and according to the state statutes where the loss occurred.

ANYONE LIKE THAT ON YOUR TEAM?

The insurance company has forensic engineers at its disposal, who will make engineering inspections and write reports for them.

ANYONE LIKE THAT ON YOUR TEAM?

The insurance company has forensic accountants at its disposal. These are accounting experts who can evaluate a complicated loss, like a luxury home or a business income loss.

ANYONE LIKE THAT ON YOUR TEAM?

The insurance company has personal property replacement companies at its disposal. These companies give super low prices to insurance companies on everything from automobiles to electronics to jewelry, and everything in between. You'll probably have to pay retail.

ANYONE LIKE THAT ON YOUR TEAM?

The insurance company has salvage companies at its disposal, in order to take damaged goods and sell them, thereby recovering some of the money the insurance company paid in your claim.

ANYONE LIKE THAT ON YOUR TEAM?

The insurance company has private investigators at its disposal. These people will perform background checks, neighborhood interviews, public records searches, even conduct surveillance of YOU at home and at work.

BUT, WHO <u>DO</u> YOU HAVE ON YOUR TEAM?

DO YOU EVEN <u>HAVE</u> A TEAM?

DO YOU THINK THAT YOU MAY BE AT A HUGE DISADVANTAGE?

<u>Keep reading…your disadvantage is just about to disappear!!!</u>

FOREWORD

KEEPING PROMISES

In one way, insurance is nothing more than promises made between two parties.

In another way, it is much, much more than that. It's legally binding contract.

The insurance company writes a policy that makes commitments to you...promises.

The insurance company expects you to pay a fee, called a premium. In the policy, there are things that both of you must do, which is your way of keeping your promises.

The agent who sells you a policy makes promises about how the policy will protect you. We all hope that those promises made by the agent are actually found in the policy!

When it is all said and done, the process of filing a claim, and getting that claim paid, is the way that the promise is kept. <u>It is the essence of the insurance contract.</u>

<u>CLAIMS ARE ALL ABOUT KEEPING PROMISES.</u>

That's one of the things I like best about being a claims adjuster.

The reputation of an insurance company is usually not spoiled by charging high premiums, because few people complain if they're convinced that there's more value in the policy than the amount of money they pay.

The reputation of an insurance company is usually not spoiled by paying huge commissions to their agents, because most people couldn't care less how much money their agent makes.

The reputation of an insurance company is usually not spoiled by investing money poorly.

<u>Reputations of insurance companies are usually ruined due to poor claims handling.</u>

Insurance companies spend millions of dollars in advertising to convince you that you're better off or smarter to do business with them. They tell you how many people switched to their company last year. (They never say how many people left or got cancelled though) They want you to buy their policies and remain their customers for a long time. In the insurance business, that's called "persistency." Persistency means policies that stay on the books for a long time. Agents get bonus money when they have good persistency.

I consider it part of my job as an adjuster to make the insurance company and the agent look good. If I treat the policyholder with compassion and respect, and do everything I can to get their claim paid as soon as possible, I know that the policyholder will think positively about the insurance company and the agent that sold them the policy. I even tell the policyholders what a great agent and great insurance company they have…just so they don't miss my point.

I do this quite selfishly…I freely admit it. If the agents are happy with the way I take care of their clients, they will ask for me to be the adjuster whenever their policyholders have a claim.

I also know that the claims examiners at the insurance companies are human beings just like you and me. They love people who make their work easier, and don't love people who make their work harder. If I send them good reports that contain all the information they need to pay a claim, they can pay the claim and close the file.

For a claims examiner, cleanliness is not what's next to godliness...a closed file is next to godliness!!

For me, that kind of service to others is the some of the best and most satisfying part of the work. But, far and away the greatest satisfaction comes when my strategies help people recover thousands more dollars in their claim settlements!

But now that this book is published, my level of satisfaction is going to grow exponentially!

This entire book is about helping YOU, THE POLICYHOLDER OR CLAIMANT, maximize the amount of money you are entitled to receive from the insurance company when you have a loss.

I can't possibly help more than a few hundred people in a year. I'm only one guy in one place. However, with this book, millions around the globe will be helped getting their claims paid.

Deepak Chopra says that one of the most important things we can do for ourselves is to turn our inner dialogue from the question "What's in it for me?" to "How can I help?"

This is my greatest motivation for writing this book. I can truly envision millions of people the world over reading this book and doing the simple things it shows. I envision those millions of people collecting untold millions of dollars that they would not have collected if it were not for the strategies in this book. I am eager to receive letters and emails from people all over the world, telling me how this book made a difference in their lives.

Perhaps one of those people who write to me will be you. I'm waiting to hear YOUR story.

This book is dedicated to my Redhead, Julie. I made <u>her</u> a promise that I'd love her forever, and I'm keeping that promise. In all of my life, I've never known a more fascinating woman. I'm still amazed and thankful every day that she loves me. Thank you, Julie, for your loving patience with a guy writing his first book. Took me two years, but I did it!!

I'd also like to thank Corey Rudl of the Internet Marketing Center. Corey tragically died in an auto racing accident on June 2, 2005. But it was Corey who gave me the idea in July of 2004 to write a book about what I know best.

My sincere thanks to:

Dr. Tim Ryles, former Georgia Insurance Commissioner. Tim was so very gracious to read my manuscript and make very important recommendations.

Geri Lumsden and Bill Day for reading the manuscript and offering their expertise.

Charles Dale, VP of Operations at Jansen International, Houston, Texas, for making helpful recommendations for the chapter on Public Adjusters.

The folks at Trafford Publishing Company. They have helped make my dreams come true.

Finally, to all my readers around the globe – past, present and future. Thanks for such wonderful support. May your lives be enriched and restored, and may you achieve peace of mind and heart.

CHAPTER ONE

WATER, WATER EVERYWHERE

In this chapter, you'll learn that your insurance adjuster doesn't always know what he's doing, and the only one who is responsible for getting all the money you're owed is YOU.

In September 2005, the internal plastic water line that feeds our refrigerator's icemaker burst, and started leaking water out on the floor of the kitchen. Naturally, this happened while no one was there to see it, and was leaking behind the refrigerator. Some of the water got over to a nearby wall and got under the vinyl floor. The 40-year-old plywood underlayment acted like a sponge, and soaked up the water, causing it to buckle and swell. So, when we discovered it, I quickly closed the valve under the sink that fed the icemaker line. But the floor was already damaged and would need repair.

We called an appliance repairman, who did find the cracked line and replaced it.

And all of a sudden, we had an insurance claim.

There is a major difference between a slow leak that occurs over time and a burst water line that happens suddenly. The normal Homeowners policy will not cover the slow leak. Please refer to Chapter Thirteen, Residential Water Claims.

Here's what it says about the slow leak kind of loss in my Homeowners policy. It probably says the same thing in your policy.

Under "Dwelling and Other Structures" coverages, we do not cover loss resulting directly or indirectly from:

6. <u>Continuous or repeated seepage or leakage of water</u> or steam <u>from within a</u> plumbing, heating, automatic fire protection or sprinkler or air conditioning system or from within a <u>household appliance</u> which occurs over a period of weeks, months or years." (Underlined emphasis mine)

That means that the sudden water damage losses are covered. Your policy will say something very close to this. Read it for yourself.

I called our insurance company and reported the claim. The next day, one of their claims examiners called me to verify the damage and start the claims process. I mentioned to the examiner that I was an insurance adjuster, and that I could save them a bunch of money hiring an independent adjuster if they'd like to work with me. I offered to get a restoration contractor's estimate and send them photos of the damage. I had already written a damage estimate on the estimating software that I have in my computer. I offered to send them a copy of that estimate. Amazingly, they declined the offer, and said that they'd be giving this loss assignment to an independent adjusting company in my area.

The next day, I received a call from the local adjuster, and he made an appointment to inspect the damage the following Saturday.

When I went to the door that Saturday morning, I was greeted by a fresh-faced, clean-cut young man who announced that he was my adjuster. This young man couldn't have been more than 25 or 26 years old. I've got clothes older than this kid. I asked him about his experience in claims, and found that he'd been in claims for about three years. This was his first job out of college. He did primarily homeowners losses.

I told him that I was a General Adjuster, and he didn't even know what that meant. So, I had to explain to him that it meant I'd been a claims adjuster for a long time, had gone through a lot of schooling, and was now handling large commercial and industrial losses.

We went into the kitchen. I stood out of the way so I didn't impede his work. He measured the room and photographed the damage. I didn't point out anything out of the ordinary because I wanted to see what kind of estimate he would write without my input. After all, I was writing a book about claims, and what it takes to get paid all that a consumer is entitled to collect.

I gave him a copy of the appliance repairman's paid invoice so he could document the cause of the damage.

He explained that he would be writing an estimate and sending it to the insurance company. I asked him to send me a copy of his estimate, and he agreed to do so.

He didn't do it, though.

About a week later, I received a letter from the claims examiner at the insurance company. The letter included a copy of the adjuster's estimate and a check for $309.64.

The estimate was accurate in its measurements, but that's where the accuracy ended. The boy adjuster wrote an estimate that replaced the plywood underlayment for the part of the floor that he could see, and put down a new vinyl floor throughout the kitchen. The amount of the estimate was $1,701.94. He applied depreciation of $392.30, subtracted our $1,000 deductible and the Actual Cash Value (ACV) claim amount was $309.64.

Our Homeowner's Policy had a Replacement Cost Value (RCV) clause. Here's what the policy says about RCV at the time of a loss:

"Conditions, How losses are settled.

2. Under Dwelling and Other Structures Coverages:

We will pay only the actual cash value of the damaged property until actual repair or replacement is completed."

So, the insurance company was correct to pay the ACV up front. I had 180 days to make repairs and show that I'd spent or incurred the RCV, and collect that depreciation amount of $392.30 that they had held back.

However, let's get back to the estimate of the boy adjuster.

The plywood underlayment had swollen under about half of the kitchen floor. More importantly, it has swollen under the sink base cabinet right next to the refrigerator. The cabinets in our kitchen were custom built in place, not the kind that come in a box from your local home improvement store. All the young adjuster would have had to do to discover this was to look inside the cabinet, but he didn't. The sink base was going to have to be removed before the flooring could be repaired. But that meant the custom sink base cabinet would have to be dismantled to be removed.

The boy adjuster missed this.

Dismantling the sink base means first removing the faucet, then removing the sink, then removing the countertop. That also meant that the dishwasher on the other side of the sink base would have to be disconnected and reconnected after repairs.

The boy adjuster missed this.

The countertop was also a custom laminate. Trying to remove it would destroy it. The countertop was also glued down to the top of the base cabinets. So, new countertop of like kind and quality would be required…not just over this cabinet, but for all the countertop on the rest of the cabinets.

The boy adjuster missed this.

The cabinets were custom built when the house was built in 1970. So, the sink base cabinet would have to be custom rebuilt. We were pretty confident that a finish carpenter (no, not a carpenter from Finland) could build the cabinet to match the other cabinets perfectly. But, it would be expensive. Then, all of the cabinets would have to be repainted to match. More expense.

The boy adjuster missed this.

After I reviewed the boy adjuster's estimate, I called the claims examiner at the insurance company. I reminded him that I had offered to save him the cost of the independent adjuster. Then, I told him about all of the things that his boy adjuster had missed.

The examiner was not happy.

So, I offered again to have a local restoration contractor write an estimate for repairs, and that I'd submit that estimate to the examiner. He finally agreed. I even offered to have my contractor meet at my home with the boy adjuster and agree on an estimate. The examiner told me that wasn't going to be necessary.

The restoration contractor's accurate estimate was $5,785.45. I sent it to the examiner, and he sent me a supplemental check for another $3,897.26. The repairs got done, and I got my total holdback amount of $970.85.

Friends, this was a small loss. It does not compare to a fire, or tornado, or hurricane. But, in this one small loss, where a young adjuster didn't notice obvious things about the damages, there was a difference in settlement of $4,475.81.

Now let's say for a moment that I was an average person who had never read his homeowner's policy. Let's also say that I was not familiar with home repairs and remodeling. (Do you think that there might be TENS OF MILLIONS of people just like that?) With just those two assumptions, I would be at a big disadvantage. A person like that could receive the estimate and check from the insurance examiner, and be led to believe that those repairs were all he was entitled to collect.

The insurance company didn't offer to have my contractor meet with the adjuster and reach an agreed estimate. As a matter of fact, they declined the offer the first time. I had to get my own contractor to write an estimate.

If I had been that average guy, my lack of knowledge about the claims process….in this one small loss….could have cost me almost $4,500.00 !

Or, stated another way…by simply using the strategies in this book, I collected almost $4,500 more than the insurance company was first willing to pay. In defense of the insurance company…once I presented the correct amount of the loss, they willingly and quickly paid. But they never offered any assistance to help me make sure my claim was correct.

I didn't expect them to, and neither should you.

In defense of the boy adjuster, he seemed to be sincere, and I believe he was doing his best with the knowledge he had. I never thought for a minute that he was trying to cheat me or shortchange me.

But, now that I've defended the insurance company and the adjuster just a little…let me ask you to think about YOUR situation.

What if the adjuster that the insurance company sends to your house is as inexperienced as the one I had?

What if <u>you're</u> not very familiar with home repair, and you are forced to rely upon the mercy and goodness of the adjuster? How does it make you feel when you know you're vulnerable because of what you DON'T know?

What if your adjuster is an adjuster purposefully writes an estimate meant to save the insurance company money? The adjuster can do that in a number of ways:

1. He can use unit pricing in his estimate that is below what it actually costs.
2. He can leave out repairs and hope you don't catch it.
3. He can leave out repairs because he doesn't know what he's doing.
4. He can tell you that you have to use the insurance company's "approved contractor or vendor."
5. He can apply high depreciation.

What if your loss is after a tornado or hurricane, and your adjuster is a temporary adjuster, also known as a "Storm Trooper?" These types of adjusters have very little training and often write inaccurate estimates.

QUESTION: How are you going to protect your assets and be sure that you're collecting all the insurance proceeds you're entitled to collect?

ANSWER: By doing exactly what I tell you in this book!!!

<u>**You...and ONLY YOU**...are responsible to collect all the insurance proceeds you are entitled to collect.</u>

CHAPTER TWO

INSURANCE COMPANY GAMES AND SCAMS

Here are just a few of the actions I've seen one insurance company take to cut costs in the handling of claims. I saw these actions from the inside during the time I was a claims examiner for that company.

1. Independent Adjusters (IA). This company uses IAs from lots of different companies all over the United States. They spend many millions of dollars a year for the services of these adjusters. This particular insurance company handles about 2,500 claims every MONTH...just in their Property Insurance Department. The insurance company knows that their volume of business makes up a pretty large percentage of the income of many of these claims adjusting companies. So, the new VP of claims made a decision to renegotiate the fees that the insurer would pay to the IAs. Naturally, the amounts were reduced, not increased. In order to do this, dozens of new IA companies were hired at the new reduced rates. The assignments to the IAs on the old contracts were abruptly stopped.

Let me assure you that the new fees are so low that adjusters who get these assignments will do the very minimum effort required to settle a claim. <u>That is not good for any of their policy holders.</u>

The company also had a small number of Field Staff Adjusters scattered around the country. The company did a time and expense study, and determined that it cost less per claim to have an employee/adjuster handle it than to have an IA handle it. They also discovered that the average amount of the settlement check was lower when an employee/adjuster handled the claim. So, now the company is in the hiring mode, adding many more field staff adjusters to handle property claims around the country.

One of the big drawbacks to this change is that many of the field staff adjusters are young (and/or brand new in the business) and not adequately trained, either in interpreting the company's insurance policies, or in the adjusting process. Many of the field staff adjusters know little about construction and disaster repair. However, the new VP knows up front that the field staff adjusters don't have to be very well trained to do their job just well enough to close lots of files.

These changes, using more staff adjusters and less IAs, and paying the IAs less, will save the company millions per year in claims expenses.

2. Estimating software. In the insurance claims adjusting industry, there are lots of companies that produce estimating software. There is software for auto repair, dwelling repair, commercial building repair, contents replacement, and many other applications. The programmers use vast databases of materials costs, labor costs, geographic locations, ZIP codes, and much other data to come up with software that will figure out how much it costs to fix or replace something in your area.

As you might expect, some software is more accurate than others. Some estimating software consistently calculates a lower price for repairs of dwellings.

Can you guess where this is going?

The new VP of Claims did another study, in which he took various estimates from all over the United States and compared those estimates to the estimating software from Software Company X. Company X is ALWAYS lower in its unit prices. The study confirmed what the new VP suspected....that if our claims department and the field staff adjusters used Software Company X's estimating software, our average estimate amounts would drop by about 12%. That means that claims can be settled for a lower dollar figure.

For example, an estimate written by an independent adjuster in Iowa might have a total of $20,000.00. If someone in the claims department entered the exact same measurements and quantities into Company X's estimating software, the total might be $17,600.00.

Please remember this: The prices in EVERY company's software are just ESTIMATES...they usually don't represent how much it actually costs to complete the repairs. USUALLY, the cost to repair is higher than the estimate total.

The new VP knows something else, too. He knows that nearly every claimant will accept the insurance company's estimate...and the check that's sent to them...without question. They might not like it...they might not be able to repair or replace their property for the amount of money that the insurance company pays. Those policyholders might have to use their own money to make up the difference.

So, the new claims procedure is to use Software Company X's estimating software for all field staff adjusters. The examiners are "encouraged" to compare the estimates from other independent adjusters with Company X's database to see if the estimate can be lowered.

3. Replacement cost holdbacks. **This method of cutting costs is the most ruthless and cynical of all.**

At this insurance company, they write an all-risk dwelling policy, which only covers the dwelling and other unattached structures. There is no Contents coverage, and no Additional Living Expense like the standard HO-3 homeowners policy. All risks are covered subject to exclusions carefully listed in the policy.

(These policies are usually written through mortgage company escrow accounts. If your Homeowner insurance is paid through your mortgage company's escrow account, you might have one of these policies, and not even know it. Read Chapter Three for more details.)

Under the "Conditions" section in the policy, it tells the policyholder about the method that the insurance company pays a claim. These kinds of policies pay replacement cost valuation (RCV) on the Dwelling damages. That means that the policy pays whatever it costs to repair the property, up to the policy limits. However, the estimate for repairs is written with depreciation applied to the loss.

See Chapter Fifteen for a description of Depreciation.

For any claim greater than $1,000, the insurance company "holds back" the depreciation amount, and pays only the Actual Cash Value in the first check. Once the policyholder has made the repairs and provided proof that the repairs are completed, the insurer will release a second check for the holdback amount. The policy states that the policyholder is eligible to receive the holdback amount if the repairs are completed within 180 days of the date of loss, and a letter is sent to each policyholder stating this in clear language.

The Conditions of the policy are not the cynical and ruthless part. When any policy gives Replacement Cost coverage, the insurance companies have a right to see that the insured property is actually replaced. So, the insurance company is correct to issue a first check for the Actual Cash Value.

For example: You, the insured, had lightning strike your house, and destroy your television. The TV is five years old, and you paid $500 for it. To buy the same model TV today would cost $600. The depreciated value of that TV is $250, or half of its useful life. So, the insurance company would issue a check for $250, with the understanding that if you cashed the check and did not buy another TV, you would not have made a replacement. However, if you do buy another TV for $600, and send the insurance company a copy of your receipt, they would send you another check for $350.

See how that works? That part is OK, and completely fair. <u>It's the rest of this story that will make you mad.</u>

At this insurance company, the average size of all claims is about $4,000. The average holdback amount is about $800. For the first year or so that I worked there, we did not holdback any amount less than $1,500. That larger amount of holdback occurred on the larger losses, like heavy fires or total losses. The claims managers had made the decision that it made the examiners' jobs easier to not have to reopen a closed file and pay a holdback on the smaller claims.

Remember, this company's claims department handles about 2,500 claims per month. You can see that just the average holdback amount runs about $2 million a month, or over $24 million per year.

The new VP of Claims did another study about the holdbacks. He discovered that less than 50% of the policyholders who were eligible to receive a holdback amount ever actually contacted the insurance company and requested that holdback. The policyholders usually didn't understand the letter they were sent which explained the holdback procedure, and didn't call to get an explanation.

So, another new procedure was put into place. The claims examiners were instructed to go back to applying the depreciation amount for any loss over $1,000, just like it said in the policy.

The new VP of Claims figures he'll save the company another $15 million per year just on this one change alone.

At no time did the VP ever suggest that the policyholders receive another letter after their claim had been settled to remind them that they still had a certain amount of money they may be eligible to collect. Oh, no! Perish the thought!! On the contrary…the Vice President demonstrated that his loyalty is to the profitability of the insurance company…just as it should be.

Now, don't you imagine that these kinds of cost-cutting measures are everyday occurrences in MOST of the insurance companies' claims departments? I am not suggesting that the claims departments should be operated inefficiently. I am not suggesting that the insurance companies don't have the right to make business decisions that favorably affect their profitability.

What I AM saying is that two of these three examples increased the profitability of this one insurance company by REDUCING THE AVERAGE SETTLEMENT AMOUNT OF CLAIMS!!! This company is actually cheating its own policy holders out of millions of dollars that the policyholders could be collecting…SHOULD be collecting…but WON'T be collecting.

It's perfectly legal…but, in my opinion, highly immoral! What kind of people purposely cheat their own customers…all the while telling the public about how fast their claims are settled?

And the insurance company did it relying upon the ignorance of their customers…the policyholders!!!

What should you learn from this? Ask your self these questions:

Are you really "in good hands®?"

Is your insurance company really "on your side®?"

Is your insurance company "like a good neighbor®?"

CHAPTER THREE

YOU'RE FIRED!
YOU DID YOUR
JOB TOO WELL!

Can you imagine that this could happen to you? It did happen to me...here is my true story.

<u>There is an extremely important strategy for you, the homeowner, in this chapter.</u>

It is really important that you read this chapter all the way through. If you have your homeowners insurance premium paid by your lender out of an escrow account, THIS STORY WILL SHOCK YOU. IF YOU ARE NOT <u>VERY CAREFUL</u>, YOU COULD END UP WITH <u>NO COVERAGE</u> ON YOUR HOUSE. Or, you could end up with inferior coverage at four times the price...<u>without your consent!!</u>

Please read on…it's going to take a little work to get to the shocking part. Hang with me.

In the last chapter I told you how I worked for a couple years as a claims examiner at the home office of an insurance company. But it was not just a normal property insurance company. This company sells hazard insurance to mortgage companies and banks in the United States. Let's call this company…"ABC." (That's not its real name, nor is it the initials for its real name.)

You or I could not buy one of these policies, even if we wanted to. Why? Because ABC's customers are the mortgage lenders.

A lot of people who have a mortgage have an escrow account with their lender. Part of each monthly mortgage payment goes into that escrow account to pay for insurance and/or property taxes. Escrow accounts are very popular with homeowners because the bank becomes responsible for paying the premium to the insurance company, and paying the property tax bill to the county. The borrower writes one check per month, and forgets about it.

But there are a lot of problems with escrow accounts.

Sometimes, the mortgage companies sell their mortgages in big portfolios to other lenders. When that happens, the buyer gets all of that escrow money, too. In the confusion surrounding the sale of those mortgages, and the time it takes to do the deal, the buyer sometimes fails to make premium payments on time. When that happens, some policies occasionally get cancelled.

Sometimes, people don't automatically renew their policies that are in escrow, and the policies cancel.

Sometimes, insurance companies cancel homeowner policies, and the borrower doesn't tell the lender, or replace the coverage in a timely manner. Sometimes, the insurance companies send the cancellation notices only to the lender, and the homeowner never knows his policy was cancelled.

Sometimes, lenders just screw up and forget to make premium payments...even when the money is in the escrow account and it's no fault of the homeowner. And sometimes the lenders fail to notify the homeowner that they have no insurance. The homeowner finds out when they have a claim.

Banks and mortgage lenders have to deal with large numbers of foreclosed properties and repossessed properties, also known as REO (Real Estate Owned) properties. The borrower defaults on his loan, and there's no one to pay the insurance premium, and the policy gets cancelled. I'll come back to this in a minute.

In each of these examples, the home ends up without insurance coverage. Banks and mortgage companies do not like having loans on properties without insurance. If the house burns down, so does their equity.

ABC to the rescue!!!

ABC makes a deal with the banks and mortgage companies that it will write a policy from the date of cancellation of the borrower's coverage, and into the future...as long as a premium is paid. ABC takes all these properties sight unseen, with no underwriting. Most of the time, ABC actually back-dates the policy to the date when the other policy cancelled...even after a claim is filed.

You can imagine that this is very high risk business for ABC. They don't get a chance to look at any house, no matter if it's a mansion on the hill, or a "crack house" in the worst part of a major city. ABC accepts them all. But, because they accept this high risk business, they charge premiums that are two...three...four times as much as a standard premium.

ABC has a remarkably low loss ratio, and makes enormous profits on this line of business.

So, if you are a homeowner, and your policy gets cancelled for any reason, the bank will pay the premium for you and charge it to your escrow account. Did your house payment suddenly go up? Your monthly house payment likely went up a lot to pay for the new insurance.

The BIG problem...the HUGE problem for YOU...the homeowner...is that the bank only cares about THEIR MONEY. They don't care about you, the contents of your home, your legal liability, or where you'll live if you have a fire and can't live in that house. They usually only write the policy for <u>the unpaid balance of the loan</u>.

Lenders don't care about the replacement cost of your property. Forced-placed coverage usually only covers the outstanding loan balance on your mortgage. So, if you had a house worth $150,000.00, and a loan balance of $50,000.00, the lender would buy a policy for $50,000. The lender only cares about getting the loan paid off.

What if your house is worth $150,000.00, and your loan balance was only $50,000, and you have a total loss fire with <u>their</u> coverage?

You are going to have a very bad, life-changing experience, that's what!!

Normally, your property insurance covers your liability. Lenders don't care about your liability exposure. They don't care if a delivery man falls on your property and sues you for six figures. Forced-placed coverage only covers the outstanding loan balance on your mortgage. There is no liability coverage.

Normally, your property insurance covers your contents...your personal property, like your furniture and other belongings. Lenders do not care about your contents. They don't care if everything you own is destroyed. Forced-placed coverage only covers the outstanding loan balance on your mortgage. There is no contents coverage.

Normally, when a homeowner buys insurance to protect his home and contents, the policy also has coverage for Additional Living

Expenses. Lenders do not care if you are forced out of your home because something happens that makes your home unfit to live in. Lenders don't care if you have to live temporarily in a homeless shelter. Forced placed coverage only covers the outstanding loan balance on your mortgage. There is no ALE coverage.

Also remember that the LENDER owns the forced-placed policy on your property, not you. The settlement checks will go to them, or perhaps made payable to the lender and you. But they usually won't let you cash the check.

Are you still with me? I haven't told you yet how I got fired for being the best claims examiner in the company. What you just read was the important back story.

Here comes the rest of the story.

A big percentage of ABC's business is foreclosed properties. There are millions of foreclosed properties in America today. These houses are standing empty, and deteriorate quickly. There are so many foreclosed properties in America that a cottage industry sprung up. There are companies that manage the care of foreclosed properties, like boarding them up, cutting the grass, removing abandoned junk, and filing insurance claims for the lenders (who own the houses) when something happens.

At ABC's claims department, we dealt with these property managers on a daily basis. They were the sources of most of our claims. Some are very professional, but others who claim to be property recovery professionals regularly submit fraudulent claims. They attempt to get ABC to pay these claims. Their clients are the same mortgage companies and lenders that are ABC's clients.

If the property managers are successful in getting ABC to pay claims that it doesn't owe, the banks and mortgage lenders get more money to fix up the foreclosed houses.

So, it's actually NOT in the lender's best interest for ABC to deny claims that it does not owe. It's also NOT in the lender's best interest to make the property managers stop submitting fraudulent claims.

It's also NOT in ABC's best interest to anger or lose one of its big mortgage lender clients, because ABC is making so much money on the business.

The property managers know that the level of expertise is quite low among ABC's claims examiners (with a few exceptions…like me). The level of expertise is even lower among the company's staff adjusters, who sometimes are allowed to pay claims. So, speaking figuratively, the property managers "throw the mud against the wall, and see what sticks." Surprisingly, a lot sticks.

I investigated each claim I received thoroughly, and denied a lot of claims. In fact, during one period of about six months, I denied 89% of the claims that one property management company sent in. The average denial rate for the rest of the claims examiners was around 40% for the same time period and the same property management company.

Imagine…even the examiners with the least amount of training were denying 40% of the claims!

The denials were for a lot of different reasons. In that period of time, 29% were denied because the estimate was below the deductible. 11% were denied because the loss was not within the policy period. 11% were denied because the adjuster who inspected the dwelling found no damage. 17% were denied due to wear and tear, which wasn't covered in that policy. The rest were denied for other various reasons.

Naturally, that particular property management company went nuts. They complained to my Claims Manager, and to the VP of Claims, and to the mortgage company. Out of hundreds of claims I'd handled, they were never able to find even one claim that I'd denied in error.

But, one day both my Claims Manager and the VP of Claims got an email from the Mortgage Lender, demanding that I be removed from handling their claims.

The managers told me that I was the best claims examiner in the entire company...and they totally supported the way I was protecting ABC's money. They paid me a cash bonus because I had closed almost 1,200 claims in 2004. In the two years I worked for ABC, the managers NEVER told me to change the way I was handling claims.

But one of their biggest clients made a request, and they were going to comply.

I was fired...for doing my job better than anyone else in that company!

<u>There is an extremely important strategy for you, the homeowner, in the rest of this chapter.</u>

When I worked for that Atlanta insurance company, I regularly talked to people who said that the first time they were aware of the forced placed policy is when they filed a claim. Their old insurance company sent the premium notice to the lender, who missed the premium due date, and the policy cancelled. The lender then forced placed a policy on the property.

So, what do you do if this happens to YOU?

One of these scenarios will explain your situation:

1. <u>You</u> were negligent, and allowed your policy to lapse. It's not the lender's fault. The insurance company notifies the lender of the cancellation date. The lender forced-placed a policy for the loan balance. You have a claim.

What do you do? Very carefully follow the steps in this book to take control of your claim. Then, as soon as the claim is completed, buy your own policy and cancel the one the lender owns. Just make sure that you have coverage IN PLACE before you cancel the lender's policy.

2. The lender was negligent, and allowed your policy to lapse. Then, the lender force-placed a policy for the loan balance. You have a claim.

What do you do?   ALERT!!!!   Get an attorney involved IMMEDIATELY!! Don't wait!! Don't try to be a nice guy!!

Get your documentation in order. Make sure that you can prove it was the lender's fault that the premium was not paid. Next, have your attorney call the person at the lender who manages the Escrow Department. Explain what happened, and ask them what they plan to do to make things right. If they fix the problem and you don't suffer any loss from their negligence, then all will be well.

How does the lender fix the problem THEY created?

The bank could contact your insurance company and accept liability. Many times, the insurance company will allow the bank to make the premium payment and reinstate the policy. Once that's completed, you can proceed with your claim based upon the insurance policy that you did have before the cancellation.

The lender could accept liability and pay your claim out of their own pocket. You'll usually see donkeys flying around outside your house right before this happens.

If the insurance company will not allow the policy to be reinstated, then you must seek damages from the lender itself. Your attorney must file a lawsuit against the lender.

Watch this carefully!!

1. If you have an escrow account through your mortgage lender, make sure that your homeowners insurance policy is in force at all times.

2. Call your homeowners insurance company, and make sure that they are sending renewal notices and premium notices to you, not just your mortgage company. Too many mistakes happen too frequently to trust your mortgage lender to take care of your business.

Remember earlier in the chapter I said that hazard insurance rarely has coverage for Contents, Additional Living Expenses (ALE), or Liability? If you have a fire, and your house is full of personal property, it's worth tens of thousands. If you have a fire, and can't live in your house for a few months, ALE coverage can mean the difference in staying at a homeless shelter, and some of your kids staying somewhere else, or keeping the family together in a short term rental apartment or house. Again, tens of thousands of dollars that you should be able to collect.

If a delivery man falls on your sidewalk and is injured....and you're liable... his lawsuit for damages could easily run into six figures. Hazard insurance doesn't cover liability.

So, you cannot afford to place all your assets and your property at risk by trusting someone else to handle your money for you. You cannot just pay your monthly mortgage payment and forget it.

The strategy is to make CERTAIN that your escrow account keeps your Homeowners insurance policy in force AT ALL TIMES!

This strategy ALONE could save you, the homeowner, hundreds, perhaps many thousands of dollars of insurance benefits.

Final, final thoughts! Your mortgage contract probably states that the mortgage company will replace your coverage in the event of the cancellation of your insurance coverage. However, if the mortgage company force-places <u>an inferior policy</u>, a true "replacement" of coverage has not occurred. Point this out to your attorney. You might have a very compelling cause of action against the mortgage company!!

CHAPTER FOUR

DON'T BE IN A HURRY

This chapter will show you what to do in the first few hours and days after your loss occurs. There are some <u>crucial tips</u> below about keeping records, and hiring restoration contractors...don't miss them.

How many times have you heard an insurance company's radio or television commercial say how fast they settle claims? That really sounds good, doesn't it? Who wouldn't want their claim settled quickly?

But my experience has been that hastily settled claims are settled far below what they are worth. It's almost as if the policyholder or claimant becomes willing to give the insurance companies a big discount in return for the speed of getting a settlement check.

Don't be one of those people who are motivated by a quick settlement check.

I'm not suggesting that you should drag your feet and be uncooperative in the process. You should be very cooperative...<u>but</u>

on your own terms, not the insurance company's terms. I'm saying that if you are in control of the claims process like you should be, it will not usually be speedy.

The process will move along in a businesslike manner, but you must not allow yourself to be rushed into a settlement. Even if the insurance company sends you a check before you're ready to settle, you're not required to cash it.

Let's look at the first 24-48 hours after you have a loss. It really does not matter if your loss is small or large or a jumbo catastrophic disaster. It does not matter if your loss is a property loss…like a hurricane or tornado or fire, or a casualty loss…like an automobile accident. There are some things that you must do to protect yourself, your family and your property.

FIRE   OR   CATASTROPIC   WINDSTORM (HURRICANE/TORNADO) CLAIMS

FIRST THING TO DO IS TO CONTROL THE SITUATION

1. Make sure everyone is safe and accounted for…including the pets.

2. Get medical attention for anyone in the family that needs it…including the pets.

3. Contact your public utility companies. Have them send out a technician to shut off the water, power and gas immediately. That itself will increase the safety factor in your damaged dwelling.

Speak with the Fire Marshall and the local Building Inspector regarding the safety of the dwelling. You want to be sure it's safe for you to enter the dwelling after the loss. If it is not safe, don't go in there…no matter what. You can replace STUFF, but you cannot replace YOURSELF.

AFTER THE UTILITIES ARE SHUT OFF, AND BEFORE

THE RESTORATION COMPANY BOARDS UP THE
DWELLING…SAFELY do the next step.

4. Camera work

Get hold of a video camera and a couple of video tapes. You
might need a floodlight or other very powerful battery-powered light.
If your dwelling is safe to walk through, take video footage of every
room in the house where there is damage. Take footage from every
angle in every room. Make sure you take footage of your damaged
contents. Shoot footage inside closets…in open drawers, inside
boxes, on bookshelves, inside cabinets, in the garage where lots of
junk is stored. Take shots of all four sides of your home from the
outside. Take footage of the debris in the yard, especially if it has
contents items that the fire department threw out in the yard.

If you can't get a video camera, then use a digital camera and take
still photos. If you can't get a digital camera, use a 35mm camera. Use
the camera in your cell phone. Heck, use disposable cameras. JUST
TAKE THE PHOTOS AND GET YOUR DAMAGES ON FILM!!

NEVER give your film negatives or original videotape to the
adjuster. Give copies of the photos and videos, if they ask for them.
Keep track of your expenses for photos and videos…you can recover
that cost.

Want to know why camera work is so important?
A. A photo is worth a thousand words.
B. Photos trigger memories, and remind you of building and
contents items that were destroyed or damaged.
C. Time is of the essence. If you're adjuster can't get to your
property for a couple days (or weeks in hurricane losses), and you
need to protect your property, you can carefully photograph the areas
that you are protecting before you cover them or alter them. That
way, you've preserved evidence of the damages.

5. Notify your relatives or closest friends of the loss. Friends and
relatives can be extremely helpful to you…but only if YOU control

what they do.

A. Do NOT take advice from your friends and relatives, unless they have experienced a loss EXACTLY like yours, and were successful in getting every dollar they were owed. If that actually happened, they probably have a copy of this book and followed my advice to the letter.

B. Friends and relatives can be great witnesses of the damage. They can help take photos and videos. They can be witnesses when you meet with the adjuster or your contractor. They can babysit for you. They can store things temporarily for you. They can take care of your pets. They can make beer runs to the store for you while you're taking care of your claim.

6. Notify the insurance company (See Chapter Five, Notify the Insurance Company). It is certainly acceptable to phone the agent or company claim department first, but be aware that many policies require you to report a claim in writing. You'll find a Loss Notice form in the Resources Section of our website that you can download for free. Make sure you know what your policy language says regarding submitting a Notice of Loss. **THIS IS CRUCIAL!!!** If you do not notify your insurance company of your loss in the way the policy says to do it, your claim could be denied.

7. Determine what it's going to take to secure your property and protect it from further loss. This is part of your responsibility in your insurance contract. If necessary, contact a disaster restoration company to board up the building, or tarp the roof, or extract the water, etc. IF YOU DO THE WORK YOURSELF, OR ALLOW OTHERS TO DO FREE WORK FOR YOU, THE INSURANCE COMPANY MAY NOT PAY YOU FOR YOUR TIME.

8. SERIOUSLY CONSIDER HIRING A PUBLIC ADJUSTER (PA) IN THE FIRST 24-48 HOURS (see Chapter Nine about Public Adjusters).

9. If you need to contact an emergency service provider or disaster restoration contractor, go to this website address: http://www.restorationcontractor.net   You can enter your ZIP

code and the website will identify a restoration contractor in your area. I just recently began building the database at that website, so if you click on it, and it's not ready yet, use the tips below.

SUPER IMPORTANT TIP!!!

A restoration contractor is very different than a general contractor. Most general contractors who do remodeling or new construction do not have the skills and knowledge that a restoration contractor has.

For one thing, the restoration contractor is very familiar with the insurance claims process, and how insurance companies pay for repairs. The restoration contractors use similar estimating software to that used by the adjusters and insurance companies. A general contractor who submits an estimate in an unacceptable form to the insurance company or adjuster just annoys them, and slows down your claim.

Another reason to find restoration contractor is that they are usually full service contractors. They will be able to do temporary or emergency cleanup and board up. They will own the equipment for drying and water damage remediation. They are familiar with the kinds of damage that fires, wind and water do to homes. Finally, they are experts at writing accurate estimates for these specific kinds of damages.

General contractors who do not make their living in insurance restoration do not have this kind of equipment and experience. Period.

You can also look in your local Yellow Pages under "Disaster Restoration," or "Fire Restoration," or "Water Damage Restoration." Look for logos that say "DKI," or "ASCR," or "AAORC."

DKI - Disaster Kleen-up International. Headquartered in Chicago, IL, is a network of the leading independent property damage restoration contractors across North America. You can ask for a referral at 888-735-0800, and also find them at: www.disasterkleenup.com

ASCR – The Association of Specialists in Cleaning and Restoration, Inc. is the leading trade association for cleaning and restoration professionals worldwide, and the foremost authority, trainer and educator in the industry. You can ask for a referral in your area at 800-272-7012, or the website: www.ascr.org

AAORC - American Association Of Restoration Contractors, is a national network of reputable and reliable restoration contractors who provide top-notch restoration services. You can call them toll free at 866-771-1525, or the website: www.aaroc.com

Call at least two restoration contractors, if possible. Ask them to meet you at your home to inspect the damage within 24 hours of the loss.

Remember this important point...there is NOTHING in your policy that requires you to get two or three estimates. Meeting two contractors is just a smart way to find one that you like best and want to work with. Check out their references, and ask them for a list of satisfied customer that you can call by phone. ONLY AFTER THE CONTRACTOR CHECKS OUT should you hire him.

10. TIME TO GET ORGANIZED

Start A File

You must create a file immediately after your loss. Go to an office supply store and buy one of those cardboard accordion-like expandable folders that can hold lots of paperwork. Even a cardboard box with a lid on it is acceptable for keeping everything inside it. You don't have to be fancy, just keep everything in one place. Your file also must be portable, so that rules out using a filing cabinet at home.

During the recovery process, place the following in your file:

A. Current copy of your policy. If you don't have a copy handy, call your agent and have him get you a copy <u>immediately</u>.

B. Copies of all written correspondences (don't forget emails) between you and ANYONE regarding your claim.

C. Phone, fax and email address record for everyone involved in the claim.

D. Photos you have taken of the damages…and the repairs. This includes videotapes or still photos of the damages that you took immediately after the loss.

E. A cassette tape of your own recorded statement about how the loss occurred. (See Chapter Twenty Five, Recorded Statements.)

F. A cassette tape recorder, batteries and spare tapes for recording EVERY conversation that you have with the adjuster, claims examiner, appraiser, engineer, attorney, contractor…ANYONE with whom you discuss this claim.

G. Receipt envelope. ALL receipts pertaining to this loss should be in that envelope. NEVER give the insurance company your original receipts. They should get copies.

H. Expense log: emergency services, living expenses, mileage, even extra child care, or boarding your pets…ANYTHING that you have to pay for that relates to this loss.

I. City, County, and State Building Code requirements in writing.

J. Copy of your state Department of Insurance statutes on Bad Faith Claims, or Unfair Claims Practices. (See the Appendix for a list of all 50 states' insurance departments, and their phone numbers. You can also find this free information at my website, <u>www.insurance-claim-secrets.com</u>).

K. Waiver of Lien forms (See Chapter Thirty, Settling Your Claim). These forms are also downloadable at the website.

L. Worker's list. A list of everyone who works on your home, who they work for, and what work they're doing. Taking their photo would be a great idea, also.

M. Professional reports, such as an Engineer report, Cause and Origin report, Fire or Police report, etc.

N. Copy of all estimates.

O. Copy of all repair contracts. NO WORK WITHOUT SIGNED CONTRACTS. Also, contractors occasionally find hidden damages that will require supplemental repair costs. YOU are responsible for these costs, even though the insurance company agrees to pay. The insurance company doesn't own your house...you do. GET IT IN WRITING.

P. Copies of any advance payment checks you receive from the insurance company.

Q. If you have a contractor, or ANYONE who works on your damaged property, get a copy of their insurance certificates that show their liability insurance is in effect. No insurance, no work. Period. You CANNOT afford to have a worker get hurt on your premises and file a claim against you for liability or medical expenses.

Keep a Journal

Buy a journal book, or just simply use a standard sized legal pad as your claims journal. This means that you should write down EVERYTHING that happens in your claim.

Write down every phone conversation: Date, time, phone number, who you talked to, what was said.

Write down every meeting: Date, time, length of meeting, people in attendance, what was discussed.

Write it down WHEN IT HAPPENS. Don't rely on your memory a few days later. You'll be sorry if you try that.

11. Meet the adjuster. (First, read Chapter Seven, Claims Adjusters.)

The following procedure is what a professional claims adjuster SHOULD DO at your first meeting:

A. Introduce himself and give you his business card.

B. Sit down with you FIRST and explain what he is about to do.

C. Find out from you if you've ever had a loss before.

D. READ YOUR POLICY WITH YOU, and answer all of your questions.

E. Explain in detail the claims process, and the steps he will be taking.

F. Explain to you, the insured, what your responsibilities are in the claims process.

G. Then, after all of that.....he should inspect your damage.

If your adjuster does NOT do all of the above, in basically that order...you must realize that you may have a problem right away.

Here's another tip about adjusters. Most adjusters are likeable people, and try their best to get along and be pleasant. Occasionally, you'll find an adjuster who is disagreeable, rude and sharp tongued. If you find that you don't get along with the independent adjuster that has been assigned to your claim, call his supervisor and request that another adjuster be assigned to this claim. Make your request politely but firmly. You do not have to take abuse and poor treatment from an adjuster. If the claims supervisor won't change the adjuster, call the insurance company and ask them to assign the claim to another adjusting company.

If you're dealing with the insurance company's staff adjuster, and getting treated badly, call his supervisor and firmly request another adjuster. If the supervisor doesn't cooperate, go to his supervisor. Keep going up the ladder until you get what you want. If none of this works, call your State Department of Insurance and file a complaint.

Many times you can meet the adjuster at your location on the same day as the loss occurred. That's the ideal situation. Some damages can be mitigated (made less severe) by the speed that cleanup begins. For example, you have an icemaker supply line that bursts while you are out, and the red oak wood floor in your dining room gets very wet. If you can get the water up off the floor, and drying equipment in the room quickly, the floor will likely not swell and buckle...and the floor can be saved. If you had to wait 1-2 days for the adjuster to arrive, the floor would likely have to be replaced at much higher cost.

At this first meeting with the adjuster, make requests for advance payments, if necessary. (See Chapter Nineteen, Advance Payments.)

If you've had a major Contents loss, like fire, smoke or water damage, you'll need to replace some of these items quickly. If you have had a loss which leaves you unable to live in your home temporarily, you'll need money to pay for hotel rooms, or temporary housing, or a short term lease for a house or apartment (Additional Living Expense coverage).

Insurance companies will make these types of advance payments to the insured when the advance is requested. They seldom offer an advance.

For Casualty Claims procedures, read Chapter Twenty Four, Collision Claims.

CHAPTER FIVE

NOTIFY THE INSURANCE COMPANY

Seems sort of obvious, doesn't it? But, there are <u>different ways </u>to notify the company that you've had a loss. And <u>when</u> you notify the insurance company can make a big difference in how your claim is handled.

The first place to look for information is on your policy. Many policies will have a telephone number listed for reporting a claim. However, I've seen policies that require the policyholder to notify the company in writing. So, make sure that the method of reporting your claim is acceptable to the insurance company. Likely, your agent has his name and telephone number on the policy. If so, call him and report the loss also.

Sometimes, an agent will have settlement authority to handle small losses, such as homeowner's losses under $2,000.00. In that kind of instance, the agent could handle the claim for you. I've found this situation to be rare, though. Occasionally, captive agents (agents that work for only one company, like State Farm or Allstate) will have a small amount of settlement authority.

The first thing you should remember is that the agent is a salesperson. It's not his job to handle your claim, but to assist you in buying the coverage that's right for you. Agents can be very helpful by making calls on your behalf if you're having problems in your claim. They can be helpful in finding out key names and phone numbers for insurance company personnel that are handling your claim. If the agent has a large number of policyholders with that company, and his clientele represents a large amount of premium to that insurance company, it can be very helpful to have the agent call on your behalf when you're having problems.

After all, it's all about customer service, and keeping the promises in the insurance policy.

Sometimes, the agent or an office secretary/customer service representative will fill out a claim form (called an ACORD form), and submit the claim form to the insurance company on your behalf. In this age of the Internet, frequently the claim form is electronic, and the agent will submit the electronic form by computer.

If the agent notifies the company on your behalf, and uses some type of form, ask the agent to send you a copy of the completed form. Then, you'll be certain that the claim was submitted, and the date the claim was submitted.

Many times, however, the agent will have to refer you to the claims department of the insurance company. Your policy may have a telephone number for the claims department listed on the policy, and instructions how to make a claim.

Your policy requires you to notify the insurance company "in a timely manner" after you've had a claim. What is timely? It varies policy to policy. But each state has statutes of limitation that limit the amount of time after a claim occurrence that a claim can be made. Check with your state's Department of Insurance to determine the statute of limitation where you live...or where the loss occurred.

You'll find a list of all of the Insurance Departments of all 50 U.S. states and their phone numbers in the Appendix, and at the website at: **www.insurance-claim-secrets.com** .

For example: you live in Minnesota, and own a retirement home in Florida. The Florida house gets hit by a hurricane. The statutes for Florida would apply.

WARNING: If you wait more than a month after your loss to notify the insurance company, they will be instantly suspicious. In those cases, you should expect to receive one of two forms from the insurance company before they begin their investigation of the loss:

1. Non-Waiver Agreement. This basically states that the insurance company is going to do a thorough investigation of the claim, but that their investigation does not commit them to pay the claim. It states that they do not waive any of their rights under the policy, and that the insured does not waive any of his rights by cooperating with the investigation. The insurance company wants the insured to sign this form. However, if the Insured refuses to sign the form, the insurance company will send him a....

2. Reservation of Rights letter. This states basically the same thing as a Non-Waiver Agreement, but the Insured does not have to sign it.

Don't forget to write in your claim journal the date, time, who you spoke with, the phone number you called, and what was said when you reported your claim. That information could be very valuable later if you have problems with your claim.

Most likely, you'll receive a claim number from the company when you report the loss. Write the claim number in your journal!!! Don't expect the insurance company to quickly send you a form that has the claim number on it. Sometimes, it may be many days before the claims department sends you any correspondence, and you will likely need to speak with them before then.

WARNING: What about a situation in which someone else is at

fault, and you're making a claim against the other person's insurance company? This could happen in an auto accident, or if someone causes damage to your house, or your contents. EVEN IN THIS SITUATION, you must notify your own insurance company that you're involved in a claim.

The reason is that third party claims don't always turn out well for you, the claimant. Sometimes, the other person's insurance company denies liability or denies coverage. Sometimes, the other person's insurance company drags the process out. Sometimes, the other person's insurance company makes a settlement offer far below the fair value of the claim. Months may pass, and you have suffered a financial loss that is not getting paid.

What if you, or someone in your family, is injured in the claim…and the other guy's insurance company won't accept liability?

Those things might occur weeks or months after a loss. In many cases, you can short-cut that process and make a claim against your own insurance policy to repair the damages. Then your insurance company will do something called "Subrogation." That is, they will pay your claim, and then contact the other person's insurance company and demand reimbursement, including your deductible.

So, if you don't report your claim right away, the policy might allow that insurance company to deny your claim based upon late reporting.

Besides, your policy REQUIRES you to notify the insurance company "promptly" after you have a loss of covered property. That requirement is there no matter who is at fault for the damages.

Don't get caught in this technicality. Don't lose your right to collect what you deserve.

CHAPTER SIX

SHOULD I GET A LAWYER?

YES!!

YES!!

YES!!

Remember this important statement:

Not knowing your rights is the same as not having them.

This chapter is likely to be somewhat controversial. I've read and researched a lot to write this book. I've read other authors of how-to claims books, and they're pretty evenly split on this issue. Some think that the average person who gets real well prepared can handle his own claim without an attorney, and sometimes I agree with that. If I didn't, there wouldn't be much use in me writing this book. Many trial lawyers think that nearly everybody needs an attorney in a claims situation. I disagree with that.

Both sides have valid points. Here's what I believe.

I believe we live in a very litigious country. That's another way of saying that people file suit against each other a lot in this country. I believe that you must protect yourself and your family.

I believe that what you don't know can hurt you...it could even change the course of your life for the rest of your life. I believe that your lack of knowledge about the claims process could change the destiny of your children's lives and generations into the future. Certainly it won't change your life that much if you just have a small claim. But, if you have a major property loss, or a major liability loss, your life could be very adversely affected. You could be financially ruined.

An insurance policy is a legal contract. The insurance company agrees to do certain things and charges you a fee, called a premium. The policyholder (that's YOU) agrees to the terms and conditions of the contract. You usually don't have a choice in the terms and conditions. You either accept them or go find another insurance company. Problem is, most insurance policies are written on the same industry standard forms, so the next insurance company will likely have the same policy language.

I believe that you work too hard to be taken advantage of by an insurance company. The insurance companies have lots of attorneys on their payroll to represent their interests, and will not hesitate to consult them in the settlement process of your claim. Therefore, why should you go through the claims process without benefit of legal counsel? If you send the insurance company a document and ask them to agree to it and sign it, you can be assured that their attorneys are going to look it over before anyone signs the form. Why should it be different for you, the policyholder or claimant?

I believe that every person who files an insurance claim for anything should CONSULT an attorney BEFORE FILING THE CLAIM. This does not mean that you retain the attorney. Customarily, there is no charge for a first visit to an attorney for a consultation, either in person or by phone. But, even if it costs you money to consult an attorney, consider the fee a cost of living your life. But, every person should make informed decisions in their lives, and I do not believe that a person can make a truly informed decision about filing an insurance claim without FIRST consulting an attorney.

To move ahead in a claim without legal advice is to take the chance of relinquishing some of your legal rights. To move ahead in a claim without legal advice is to take the chance of not being paid hundreds or perhaps thousands of dollars that you could be eligible to collect.

"Hey, wait a minute!" I hear one of you say. "I had a car accident and I ran into another vehicle, and I was at fault. My insurance company is going to defend me. It's written in my insurance policy. I don't need a lawyer...the insurance company is furnishing me a lawyer."

Allow me to help you think this through.

Who is hiring the attorney to represent you? The insurance company is!

Who's paying the attorney fees? The insurance company is!

Who is the attorney really representing? The insurance company!!

The insurance company is potentially liable to pay a claim for you up to the policy's liability limits. This could cost them $50,000...$250,000...$500,000...$1 million.

So, whose money are they going to be paying out? THEIRS...NOT YOURS.

They are defending you in your liability claim because IT IS IN THEIR BEST INTEREST TO DEFEND YOU. If they defend you successfully, it will cost THEM less money.

But what if their interests are not your best interests? Who wins? NOT YOU.

<u>I believe that you must consult the right attorney</u>. Don't tell me about your brother or uncle who practices labor law for some corporation. Don't tell me about the lawyer who goes to your church...the one who practices real estate law or handles divorce cases. You need an attorney who knows insurance contract law.

<u>I believe that you should NEVER sign ANY KIND OF DOCUMENT OR CONTRACT without having an attorney review it first.</u>

Let me urge you to find an attorney who knows insurance contract law. There are many attorneys who make a fortune representing the insurance companies, but they are not the attorneys who will represent you. Look for a personal injury attorney in your area. Personal injury attorneys usually spend their time negotiating with insurance companies, and filing suit against insurance companies, so they have to be pretty familiar with insurance contact law.

Personal injury attorneys will work on a contingency fee in some cases. That means that they make an agreement with you that they will receive a percentage of your insurance settlement if they're successful in getting a settlement for you. Just remember a couple things:

1. The percentage is ALWAYS negotiable...before you sign a contract.
2. It doesn't usually make sense to hire a personal injury attorney on contingency for a property claim. Attorneys would usually want a much higher percentage of your claim settlement than even a Public Adjuster would. You might just choose to pay him an hourly rate to represent you. That would still be worth it!
3. Talk with two or three attorneys before you choose one.

4. Ask your friends for referrals. They may know a successful personal injury attorney.

5. Even if you decide not to retain an attorney on a contingency basis, have your attorney review EVERY document before you sign it.

6. DO NOT EVER agree to give a recorded statement to the insurance company or adjuster without your attorney present. It would be best to do the statement in your attorney's office. But even if it is just a three way phone call, and not done in the attorney's office, you need your attorney to be involved. Read Chapter 25.

In closing, a few thoughts about legal representation that you should know:

1. If you actually hire an attorney to represent you, the adjuster must stop communicating with you, and begin working with your attorney. If you have an attorney representing you, and the adjuster calls you, give him your attorney's phone number and address. Then, don't talk to the adjuster or insurance company after that.

2. Most adjusters don't care if an attorney is involved in your claim. In fact, many times they're glad, because they don't have to deal with the insured any more. If you're doing the things I'm recommending in this book, you're going to be exactly the person they don't want to deal with, because you're being so demanding.

3. If the insurance company and the adjuster know you're consulting with your attorney during the claims process, and that you won't sign anything without your attorney's blessing, they will be more careful about what they do. They know you are not a pushover.

4. Sometimes, the insurance companies or adjuster take it as a personal insult that you've retained an attorney. Sometimes, they drag out the process or make it harder for you. Just be aware that this happens sometimes. Also be aware that every state in the USA has an Insurance Department, and there are laws on the book dealing with Unfair Claims Practices. If you want more information about every state's Insurance Department, go to my website at www.insurance-claim-secrets.com and click on Resources. The list of all 50 states' Department of Insurance is also in the Appendix of this book.

SPECIAL MESSAGE FOR RESIDENTS OF USA AND CANADA!

I believe that many people make decisions about protecting their rights based upon their finances. Naturally, for most of us, our pockets are not that deep, and the first question we'll want to ask an attorney is, "How much is this going to cost me?"

The bottom 10% of the population has Legal Aid, or some other government program to provide them legal representation. The top 10 % of the population...the wealthy...keep attorneys on retainer and consult them often. That leaves the middle 80% of the population pretty vulnerable when it comes to legal representation.

For those of you who live in the United States or Canada, there is an excellent solution available to solve the problem of AFFORDABLE legal representation. The solution is a legal services membership, and the company is Pre-Paid Legal Services, Inc. If you'd like to learn more about it, please go to my website at: www.insurance-claim-secrets.com, and click on the button marked "Equal Access." That will show you a short streaming video presentation, and give you an opportunity to become a member of the service if you have an interest.

If you do not have access to a computer and a website, and would like to learn more about this program, please send me an email at: russlongcore@gmail.com and I'll send you more information.

And yes...if you become a member, I get a commission.

Not knowing your rights is the same as not having them.

CHAPTER SEVEN

CLAIMS ADJUSTERS

A professional, intelligent, honest adjuster is a pleasure to work with. He treats you with respect and gives his best effort to complete his investigation as quickly as possible. He is patient, knowing that you are not familiar with the claims process. He understands how upset you might be about your claim. He senses that you have already been frightened by the loss itself, and now may be frightened about the claims process.

He explains the process to you before he begins it, and invites you to be an active participant, not a spectator. He sits down with you and reads your policy with you, and explains it as he goes. He makes sure that you have his contact phone numbers, so you can get your questions answered when he's not there. He answers his phone messages promptly.

The professional claims adjuster must have empathy for people. I'm not sure if that is a skill that can be taught with a book or a class. Some of the empathy must come from a person's upbringing. Compassion for another human being who is hurting or afraid must come from deep within a person. Even having said this, it is not unusual for a person to have his compassion and empathy stretched thin by the things that happen in life.

For a moment, look at the difficult position that an adjuster is in. He is considered by the law to be in a fiduciary position. That means that he has a duty to perform. His salary or service fee is being paid by the insurance company. So, he must place the financial interests of his client or employer first in the handling of your claim. He must do his best to save money for the company in the payment of your claim. He must do his best to settle your claim for <u>the least amount of money that you will accept.</u>

At the same time, he has a duty to you, the policyholder or claimant, to complete the loss investigation in a timely manner...not stalling or procrastinating. He has the duty to help you file a claim for <u>all of the money that you are entitled to collect.</u>

BUT YOU MUST REMEMBER THIS! It is not the adjuster's <u>responsibility</u> to help you get every dollar that you are owed. That's YOUR JOB!!

Let's consider the pressures and influences that work against an adjuster, and how those pressures and influences can affect the claims process for you.

1.   Caseload. This is Number One because it's the biggest pressure in an adjuster's workday. Most adjusters I've ever known...including myself...had more cases than they could handle on a day-to-day basis. Then, a big ice storm would come through town or a severe thunderstorm with lightning and hail and tornadoes would blow through the area, and the claims would pile up. There were lots of times that I would look at 12-15 losses per day after a big storm. Normally, I might look at 1-3 losses a day. So, you can see how simple volume of cases can affect the handling of your claim.

The insurance companies and adjusting companies would rather employ overworked adjusters than underworked adjusters. It's cheaper for them in the long run.

2.   Work experience and training.   Insurance companies and adjusting companies are the same as other big corporations. They know that it costs them far less in salary and benefits to hire a young person than it costs to keep an old seasoned veteran claims adjuster. The old guy has lots of experience and training, and expects to be compensated for it. Consequently, staffing a claims department or adjusting company can be a decision made by managers for economic reasons.

I guess that's a fancier way of saying that sometimes you will get an adjuster who's not trained well enough to handle your claim. Let me give you an example from my own claims adjusting experience.

I had previous experience as a carpenter, then as a builder and general contractor. I know how to build pretty much any kind of building. I've worked with the tools, from shovels to welders to drafting tables to laser levels. I've operated bull dozers, cranes, front end loaders and fork lifts. I know how to read blueprints, how to draw blueprints for a building, and have built two houses with my own hands. In addition to that, I was a property and casualty insurance agent for many years. That's the kind of experience I brought to the claims adjusting business.

Most of the adjusters I've ever known did not have that kind of experience. Many got hired right out of college with their shiny new business degrees, and didn't know one page of an insurance policy from another. The companies they worked for had to spend thousands of dollars and many years sending them through claims adjusting schools. I'm not saying there's anything wrong with that. Getting training is a very good thing. But these young adjusters are not sitting in the bullpen studying their books, waiting for a call to go into the game (forgive the baseball analogy). They are handling claims while they learn. A BIG part of the learning process IS handling claims.

When these young adjusters write estimates, they do the best that they can. But many of them really don't know what it takes to repair a house badly damaged by fire or a tornado or a flood. So, their estimates are just that…estimates. It is very difficult for an insured to find a contractor that will agree to do the work in the estimate for the price that the adjuster's estimate shows. That's because it's priced too cheap, and/or they leave out things that will eventually have to be included in a supplemental payment.

Sometimes, adjusters are required to handle claims that are beyond their training and experience, and that adds to the pressure under which they work.

3. Company standards and Department of Insurance statutes. Every insurance company has performance standards that must be met by their adjusters. Sometimes it revolves around the number of files he handles on a monthly basis. Sometimes it is how many files he must close per month. In independent adjusting companies, an adjuster is scrutinized on the amount of billing he submits in a month. That usually determines part of his compensation.

In addition to those pressures, the adjuster must comply with Department of Insurance law regarding Unfair Claims Practices and Bad Faith Claims statutes. There are certain things that the adjuster must do to be in compliance, and some of those things have a time limit on them. In some states, penalties for non-compliance can mean jail sentences and big fines.

4. Adjuster experiences.
    A. Negative experiences. Adjusters interact with people at a very stressful time in their lives. Some people don't handle that stress very well. Many of those stressed-out people are simply afraid, and take it out on others. When the claims process is not going the way the insured expects it to go, even if his expectation is reasonable, he might say some pretty unkind things to the adjuster. Over a period of years, that can wear on an adjuster and he might get pretty defensive up front.
    B. Fraud. Adjusters who have been in the business for a while have seen lots of cases in which the insured/claimant inflates the value of the claim. The adjuster has seen some public adjusters and some personal injury attorneys inflate the value of the claim. A

seasoned adjuster develops a sense about whether a claim is valid or not. But, over time, this can lead to an adjuster becoming cynical about everyone who files a claim.

C. Policyholder/claimant ignorance. When I use the word "ignorance," I mean "lack of facts or lack of knowledge." It doesn't mean lazy or stupid. Remember the reason I wrote this book. People do not read their policies. People regularly think that they have coverage for some loss that is not covered in their policy. People do not like to hear that their claim is not covered, and the first person to hear their displeasure is the adjuster.

D. Adjuster attitude. I absolutely love the insurance claims business. I've loved it since the day I got into it. I love helping people and getting paid well to do so. I believe that most people are honest and want to do the right thing.

However, there are lots of people in the claims industry…just like in your business…that don't like their job. Some adjusters have a very cynical, negative attitude about policyholders and claimants. Some adjusters think that everybody is trying to submit fraudulent claims. Some adjusters dislike their job so much that they make everybody around them miserable. I hope, for your sake, that you do not ever meet this kind of adjuster. He can make the claims process a living nightmare.

Adjusters are actually taught in beginners' claims schools to "control" the insureds and claimants. An adjuster can actually get into trouble with his claims manager if he loses control of his insureds and claimants.

What do they consider "losing control?"

Insureds and claimants who don't just accept a settlement…or get an attorney…or get a public adjuster…or are very demanding…are considered out of control.

So, I'm actually trying to train you to be OUT OF

CONTROL...THEIR CONTROL. I want YOU to be in control!

Let's talk about the concept of "fairness", and what the word "fair" means in claims. When my children Melissa, Russ and Jarrett complained about something in life not being fair, I always told them that "fair is a place where you take your pig to win a blue ribbon." What I mean is that life is not fair, and they need to get used to it now.

In the claims business, here's a statement that might shock you:

WHAT YOU THINK IS FAIR AND WHAT THE CLAIMS ADJUSTER THINKS IS FAIR IS USUALLY NOT THE SAME THING.

Most states have statutes having to do with so-called "Fair Claims Practices." That usually means that the insurance companies have to deal honestly and promptly with the insured or a claimant. Woe unto an insurance company or a claims adjuster that does not treat the insured or claimant honestly and promptly!

You can find out more about "Fair Claims Practices" at your state's Department of Insurance. Look in the Appendix of this book, or go to: www.insurance-claim-secrets.com for more details.

COMPANY ADJUSTERS, or "STAFF ADJUSTERS"

Many insurance companies have their own claims handling personnel, known as "staff adjusters" or "claims representatives." They are employees of the insurance company, and represent the interests of the insurance company in handling your claim.

Many times, the company adjusters will have the ability to write a settlement check to pay your claim.

Don't ever forget that the staff adjusters work for the insurance company. They'll probably be friendly and professional. But it is their job to settle a claim for as small an amount of money as the insured or claimant will accept.

If you get assigned a staff adjuster by your insurance company, interview him or her and find out how many months or years of experience in claims that person has. Remember that your insurance policy does not have even one word in it that requires you to accept whatever adjuster the company assigns to your case.

If your adjuster has less than two years experience, I'd recommend asking for another adjuster.

If you meet your adjuster and don't have a good feeling of trust, I'd recommend asking for another adjuster.

If you meet your adjuster, and just don't like him or her personally, I'd recommend asking for another adjuster.

If your claim is a property claim, remember that you also can retain a Public Adjuster to assist you. See Chapter Nine, Public Adjusters.

If your claim is a casualty claim (like an auto accident), you should speak with a Personal Injury Attorney, with the understanding that you may need to be represented. See Chapter Six, Should I Get a Lawyer? and Chapter Twenty Four, Collision Claims. Also look on my website for more information about legal representation.

INDEPENDENT ADJUSTERS

The greatest majority of insurance companies will have a claims department that handles its claims, and will use independent adjusting companies to act as their eyes and ears. This simply means that the independent adjuster will investigate the claim and report his findings back to the claims department at the insurance company. Seldom do independent claims adjusters have settlement authority, but can make recommendations to the claims examiner on what course of action might be taken to settle the claim. Occasionally, the insurance company claims examiner will give the independent adjuster authority to settle a claim, and will authorize the adjuster to negotiate up to a certain dollar limit. If the adjuster can settle the loss for that amount or less, fine. Any demand that goes beyond that dollar limit will likely be reviewed and settled by a claims manager.

I'm going to repeat, almost verbatim, what I said about Staff Adjusters.

If you get assigned an independent adjuster by your insurance company, interview him or her and find out how many months or years of experience in claims that person has. <u>Remember</u> that your insurance policy does not have even one word in it that requires you to accept whatever adjuster the company assigns to your case.

If your adjuster has less than two years experience, I'd recommend asking for another adjuster.

If you meet your adjuster and don't have a good feeling of trust, I'd recommend asking for another adjuster.

If you meet your adjuster, and just don't like him or her personally, I'd recommend asking for another adjuster.

If your claim is a property claim, remember that you also can retain a Public Adjuster to assist you. See Chapter Nine, Public Adjusters.

If your claim is a casualty claim (like an auto accident), you should speak with an attorney with the understanding that you may need to be represented. See Chapter Six, Should I Get a Lawyer? and Chapter Twenty Four, Collision Claims. Also look on my website for more information about legal representation.

CHAPTER EIGHT

DANGEROUS LIAISONS

Friends, I am a firearms enthusiast. I enjoy shooting pistols, rifles and shotguns as a sport. I even like BB guns, compound bows and crossbows. It is very satisfying to be able to hit a paper target from a significant distance. It's also satisfying to be able to shoot accurately at very close range.

It's really all about math. Calculating the distance to a target and how to dial in a rifle scope so the bullet hits a target many hundreds of yards away is mathematic in its precision, but there's still an art to it.

I liked hunting when I was a kid. But, now I'm just a guy who likes shooting at the shooting range.

My interest in firearms goes much deeper than just as a sport, however. I believe that the right to keep and bear arms is a fundamental natural right. That is the right to defend one's life, liberty and property. The fact that the American Constitution has a Second Amendment that prohibits (supposedly) the Federal Government from infringing that natural right is just icing on the cake.

I am seldom without a firearm on my person. Yes, I have a concealed weapons permit.

I find myself in remote areas occasionally. I find myself in very dangerous parts of large cities on occasion. These three stories happened early in my claims adjusting career. They are all related to a certain insurance company that insured vacant and foreclosed dwellings.

The first incident happened in a very cold morning in January in Atlanta. I had an assignment to inspect fire damage in an abandoned house in a certain neighborhood in Atlanta not exactly known for its mansions. I had a key to the front door. I got to the house and placed my pistol in its holster on my right hip. I picked up my big flashlight, camera and clipboard and headed for the house. I turned the key in the lock and walked in.

I announced loudly that I was a claims adjuster, just in case someone was inside. No answer. I began writing down and photographing the damages I saw. Then, I came to a bedroom door that was mostly closed. The hair on the back of my neck stood up. I pulled my pistol from its holster and kicked the door.

In the middle of the room was what looked like a pile of moving van quilts. But when I shined my light on it, the pile moved. I shouted that I was just a claims adjuster, not a cop, and that I was just looking at damages. The guy under the quilts said "OK". I took one photo of that room, and backed out all the way to the front door. I got in my car and left.

Next incident was on the other end of the same street, southwest side of Atlanta. This time it was blazing hot Atlanta summertime. I was supposed to inspect a vacant old Victorian house. The property sat right next to a national hamburger chain restaurant. I parked my car in the restaurant parking lot and started to gather my stuff. Before I could get out of my car, I saw two men walk out of the front door of the house like they owned the joint. I picked up my cell phone and called Atlanta Police.

I told the 911 operator what I was supposed to do, and that I suspected that more people might be in the house. She dispatched a patrol car to the location, and about five minutes later, the officer pulled his cruiser up next to my car. He said that he would go to the house first and check for squatters. I asked him if he had backup and he did not. I showed him my permit and my pistol, and offered to back him up. He accepted and we inspected the house. Fortunately, we did not find any other "residents" that day.

Last incident happened that same summer, after a violent storm damaged a foreclosed vacant dwelling in the same neighborhood in southwest Atlanta. I had to inspect the roof for wind damage, so I got my stuff together with my folding ladder and headed for the front door.

I stood my ladder up to the eave and climbed up. I began measuring the roof and making a roof diagram. Suddenly, I heard someone shouting to me from the ground. I went over to where the ladder was, and found a group of four teenaged boys at the bottom of my ladder. One of them told me that they would not remove my ladder and leave me on the roof if I'd just toss down my wallet.

So, I slowly reached my right hand back and drew my pistol. I showed it to the friendly young men and suggested that they put some distance between themselves and my ladder. They politely and rapidly obliged, and I did not see them any more that day. I hurried about my business and left.

You might be horrified that I would point my gun at teenagers. But I watch the news just like you do, and see news stories of middle-school-aged kids with guns, and "drive-by" shootings. I know that a 14 year old boy with a .22 pistol can shoot me just as dead as an adult can.

I stopped taking assignments from that insurance company. I

figured that they didn't pay me nearly enough to take the chance of getting shot to inspect vacant houses.

And you wonder why some claims adjusters get grumpy after a while?

CHAPTER NINE

PUBLIC ADJUSTERS

Public adjusters get their own chapter in this book. I love Public Adjusters.

A public adjuster (PA) is an adjuster that assists an insured who has had a loss in the preparation and presentation of the insurance claim. PAs perform very valuable services to the insured by consulting with the insured on options available in their recovery, filling out forms, helping prepare inventory lists, preparing estimates on structural damages, helping to find you a temporary place to live if you're home is too damaged to live in, assisting in negotiations for settlement...and many more vital functions.

Public Adjusters work only on losses that involve property, such as homes, businesses and public buildings. Those are called "first party property claims."

If you have a loss to your property that was caused by someone else, that is called a "third party property claim." An example is when a vehicle runs into a dwelling, causing damage. In some situations, PAs will accept clients for third party losses. However, PAs cannot directly negotiate a third part claim. They can either advise the client as to the extent and value of the third party loss, or work with an attorney in presenting the claim.

Public Adjusters do not handle Bodily Injury (Casualty) losses, such as happen in an automobile accident. For assistance in those kinds of losses, consult a personal injury attorney.

There's an easy way to understand the function of a Public Adjuster. Compare them to an attorney in a lawsuit, or a Certified Public Accountant or tax preparer when filing your tax forms with the Internal Revenue Service.

Let me ask you some questions:

If someone filed suit against you, would you represent yourself in court? Or, would you just call the plaintiff and say, "You've already got a lawyer. Why don't we just use yours?" Neither choice protects you, does it?

Would you allow the IRS to prepare your tax return for you? If you did, would you expect the IRS to do its best to find every tax deduction for you so that you paid the least tax or got the biggest refund?

Do you file your own tax returns, or do you hire a tax preparation professional to prepare your tax return on your behalf?

Do you hire a tax professional because:

1. You don't have time to do it yourself?
2. The IRS has written a tax code that is too complicated for a normal person to understand?
3. You usually get a larger refund, or smaller tax liability, when you use a professional...because the professional finds more deductions for you?
4. The fee you pay is usually far less than the additional money you save?

OK then...you've just found comparable reasons to use Public Adjusters.

1. You need your own experts to help you file your claim.
2. Policies are written by the insurance companies and are usually complicated and hard to understand. These policies are known as "contracts of adhesion," because they inherently benefit the author of the contract, the insurance companies.
3. Many people are not willing to take the time to learn about their policies and learn the claims process.
4. Some people are too busy with work, and family, and life, to handle their own claim...especially in the turmoil immediately after a significantly large claim.
5. Public Adjusters usually help the policyholder collect hundreds or even thousands more dollars when the policyholder submits a claim. Their fees are a very small percentage of the amount of the settlement.

PAs usually have to be licensed adjusters, and are usually regulated by the Insurance Department of your state. Some states have special licenses for Public Adjusters. Call your state's Insurance Department office to find out more information about what Public Adjusters can do in your state. You'll find contact information for the Insurance Commissioners for all US states in the Appendix of the book.

Many of the people on the insurance company side take it very personally when a policyholder hires a public adjuster. Many truly believe that the policyholder should just trust the insurance company and adjuster to do the right thing, and not ever question them.

Adjusters and insurance company personnel sometimes play games with their own policyholders when the insured hires a PA. I've heard claims examiners refuse to speak with the insured by phone, telling the insured that, now that they are represented, all conversations have to go through the PA.

However, there's nothing in your policy that states that. Public Adjusters are not attorneys, and the attorney/client relationship is not the same as the relationship between an insured and a Public Adjuster. If your adjuster or insurance company examiner tries to pull that stunt, he's just doing it to delay and cause you problems. Call his supervisor or call the Department of Insurance.

Isn't this amazing? The insurance company writes the policy, makes the rules hard to understand, and then gets mad at you when you hire someone to help you submit a claim. This would be like the Internal Revenue Service getting mad at you because you hired an accountant to help you prepare your tax return.

But it still happens, even though it makes no sense.

The environment is changing, though. Following the hurricane seasons of 2004 and 2005, a newfound respect has grown within the insurance community regarding the value and professionalism of an accredited, licensed Public Adjuster.

Why do you think that the insurance companies and adjusters are not happy when you hire Public Adjusters? There's one big reason. Usually, when a PA is involved, the dollar amount of the claim is higher than a claim without a PA.

When I first got into the claims adjusting field, the "old timers" told me horror stories about public adjuster. They told me how crooked they were, and how they grossly inflated the repair or replacement costs in claims. They told me stories of how PAs were liars and cheats and totally dishonest.

Yet, in my experience dealing with PAs in claims, from homeowner losses to large apartment building fires, to commercial and business losses, I have not met one public adjuster that I didn't like as a person. I have not met a public adjuster who acted in an unprofessional manner. I have not met a public adjuster who wasn't trying his best to make sure that his client…the policyholder who had a loss…got every dollar that was owed to them by the insurance company.

Public adjusters usually represent a client on a contingency basis. That simply means that they help present the claim documents to the insurance company and receive a percentage of the total amount of the insurance proceeds. The average percentage nationwide is 10%. The major incentive that makes the PA work hard is to help the insured get a larger settlement from the insurance company than the insured could have gotten by himself.

The PA is motivated to maximize your claim and expedite the claim adjustment process. It is a balance of making sure that the claim is packaged as completely as possible so you collect every dollar you are entitled to collect without creating unnecessary disputes with the insurance carrier. The PA does not charge for his services until after the claim is paid to you, so they are motivated to get it settled as quickly as possible. Their fee is usually all inclusive, with no additional out-of-pocket expenses. Most established Public adjusting firms can show you how their fee is absorbed in the adjustment process.

You should know that fees are negotiable with PAs. I've seen PA firms agree to substantial discounts from their standard 10% fee on huge commercial losses, and I regularly see 10% contracts on dwelling and small commercial losses. **Caveat emptor…let the buyer beware.** Just be aware that if the PA plunks down a contract in front of you with a blank space where the fee percentage is supposed to be, DON'T SIGN IT!! Negotiate the fee you're willing to pay BEFORE signing the contract. Then let your attorney review it before you sign.

Some state's Department of Insurance regulations cover Public Adjuster fees, and the maximum amounts they can charge for their services. I don't think that's any of the State's business. For the most part, states do not regulate the fees that independent adjusters charge the insurance companies. Why regulate PA fees? I believe that the policy holder and the PA should be able to set whatever fee they can agree upon.

Regardless of my opinion, you need to check with your state's Department of Insurance for this information if you're considering hiring a PA.

You've heard of personal injury attorneys being called "ambulance chasers?" Well, sometimes PAs have to be "fire truck chasers." It is quite normal for PAs to listen in to fire and police scanners and follow the fire trucks out to the location of the fire. It is quite normal for PAs to go door to door in a tornado or hurricane damaged area and solicit business. There is nothing wrong with this, since it may be the only way to contact victims after a fire or windstorm. That being said, the PA should always be professional, respecting your time and your personal situation.

A professional public adjuster can offer valuable assistance in the preparation of your claim, or even represent you in the presentation of the claim. Hiring a PA early in the claim process can help control the situation and quickly begin the recovery process. The PA can control over-zealous restoration contractors and pushy adjusters. The PA can accelerate and smooth the claim process by walking through the loss with the insurance company's adjuster so they agree on the scope of the loss. This one process can make a huge difference in how quickly your claim is settled, and many times, prevent disputes later on. You may decide that, in your situation, it makes sense to hire a PA in the first 24 hours after your loss.

If you wish to consider hiring a public adjuster, you should treat them just like you treat the adjuster and contractor. Call two or three public adjusters. Meet them, go over the details of your claim, and listen to their proposal of how they are going to represent you.

Get referrals of satisfied customers with phone numbers that you can call and verify. Then, spend the time checking them out. Call the Better Business Bureau about them. Find out if they have a good reputation.

Once you've checked them out, and if you want to retain a PA, hire the one who checks out best.

Remember what I told you in Chapter Six, "Should I Get a Lawyer?" Don't sign anything without having your attorney review the document FIRST. But, having said that, remember that there may be many things that need immediate attention, like contents removal, emergency board-up, and temporary family accommodations. This means that you should get your PA contract in front of your attorney immediately!

If you've hired a Public Adjuster, you should treat him just the same as the insurance company adjuster. See Chapter Four, Don't Be In A Hurry, with regard to writing down everything you discuss with him. Keep an accurate record of the date and time of all of your conversations, and what was discussed. Record the conversations if possible.

Insist that the PA give you copies of every document he generates on your behalf. Insist on copies of all letters and correspondences between the PA and the adjuster or insurance company.

Your PA will likely have you sign an assignment form, in which you agree to have the PA's name placed on the settlement checks along with yours.

There are only six states in the USA that <u>require</u> the PA to be included as a payee on an insurance company settlement check: Pennsylvania, New York, Virginia, Wyoming, Illinois and Kentucky. That means that if the insurance company doesn't want to be cooperative and place the PA's name on the check, they might not be cooperative unless the law requires them to do so.

In summary, the Public Adjuster will do most of the things for you that are found in this book regarding proper documentation and submission of your claim.

REMEMBER THIS IMPORTANT POINT!!

You can do all of the things that a Public Adjuster does on your behalf if you'll follow the steps I've written in this book. This will require a lot of work on your part. If you follow my recommendations, you will assuredly collect hundreds or even thousands more dollars in your claim settlement. However, in my opinion, you will collect even more money from your insurance company when you use the services of a Public Adjuster.

For those of you who do not want to expend the effort to handle your own claim from start to finish, and are willing to pay someone to do these tasks for you, then a professional Public Adjuster will perform a tremendous service for you.

I wrote about restoration contractors in Chapter Four. Here is a little extra comment about restoration contractors.

You might also see many restoration contractors drop by to see if they can help you with temporary repairs, like tarps on roofs, board-up, and contents removal. Get written estimates from them BEFORE you sign ANYTHING. They will sometimes tell you that they were sent by the insurance company (maybe true, maybe not), and that it is your responsibility to protect your property from further damage (which is true). They may tell you that they will "direct bill" the insurance company (which they may do).

Be very careful on contents removal, sometimes known as "pack out." The more contents they clean, the more money they make. The cost to clean something is a fraction of the cost to replace it. So, when the restoration contractors are involved, the claim value is reduced, which benefits the insurance company. That is why many adjusters may bring a restoration contractor with them to the loss location. Remember that many policies pay REPLACEMENT COST, and following major fires, large windstorm and water losses, most of your damaged possessions can be replaced instead of being cleaned. Every penny that goes for cleaning your contents comes from the contents limit of liability shown on your policy declarations page. So, theoretically, a substantial amount of your insurance money to replace your items could go to the restoration company to only clean the items!! If the restoration contractor cleans a bunch of your property, and you reject it as unusable, there will be less money for replacement of your property.

The contract for cleaning and restoration of your property will be between you and the contractor...not the contractor and the insurance company. MAKE SURE YOU ARE IN CONTROL!!

As I mentioned, be careful.

Finally, I recommend that you check out the National Association of Public Insurance Adjusters (www.napia.com) for a listing of accredited public adjusting firms in your state. At the website, you'll find helpful links, articles of interest, and information on how individual public adjusters are licensed and accredited through the organization.

CHAPTER TEN

HOMEOWNERS CLAIMS

Homeowners policies and Renters policies are very similar. Most of the difference is that, in a Renters policy, there is no coverage for Dwelling and Other Structures. Otherwise they work much the same.

Let's quickly go over the HO-3 policy for homeowners. The HO-4 policy is for renters.

SECTION I	Property Coverages
Coverage A	Dwelling
Coverage B	Other Structures
Coverage C	Unscheduled Personal Property (also called Contents)
Coverage D	Additional Living Expense (also called Loss of Use)
SECTION II	Liability Coverages
Coverage E	Personal Liability
Coverage F	Medical Payments to Others

The following are things to notice about each coverage:

Coverage A   Dwelling - coverage does not apply to land. However, under Additional Coverages, trees, shrubs and plants are covered for named perils.

In a lot of cases of severe storms, trees will be broken or will fall on the "residence premises" or on the dwelling. The general rule in the HO-3 policy is that the insurance company owes you $500 to get the trees off of the "residence premises" and drop them on the ground, and that's all...no matter how many trees are down.

You may wonder why I put the words "residence premises" in quotation marks. The policy does that to tell you that there is a definition for this term inside the policy. In this example, you must be aware that the term "residence premises" means your dwelling and any other structures where you live.

Don't confuse that definition with the term "insured location." That means the residence premises, other structures <u>and the ground where you live</u>.

Do you see the difference? Do you see how you might get the two confused? Why is that important?

In this example of a tree falling...did it fall in the yard or did it fall on the buildings? You might think that you have coverage for tree removal, when you might actually only have coverage to have the tree dropped off the house.

Be careful in this matter. Some Homeowners policies extend Debris Removal coverage to include removing the trees from the insured location. <u>READ YOUR POLICY!!</u>

Coverage B   Other Structures - these are unattached garages, storage buildings, playhouses, and can even include permanently installed "jungle gyms," swingsets and monkey bars. If the swingset is just sitting in the back yard, that's not permanently installed.

Coverage C   Contents - In this section there are special limits of liability for certain personal property, such as jewelry, guns, boats, trailers, silverware and many other items. The reason that there are limits on each of these items is that endorsements can be purchased to give higher limits on each of these items, and those endorsements are called "Floaters."

If you have personal items whose value exceeds the limits in the policy, call your agent TODAY and add the floaters you need.

The WORST time to find out you do not have enough coverage is after your property is damaged or stolen.

REMEMBER…contents are settled for ACTUAL CASH VALUE, NOT REPLACEMENT COST VALUE (RC). You can buy an endorsement that gives you RC on contents, and if you do not have that on your policy, CALL TODAY and get it on there. It's very inexpensive, but could mean many thousands of dollars EXTRA in case of a loss.

REMEMBER…contents DO NOT have all-risk coverage like Coverage A and B. Contents have "named perils" coverage. Become familiar with which perils are covered. They're in your policy!

Coverage D   Loss of Use, or Additional Living Expense - read Chapter Twelve about this coverage.

Coverage E   Personal Liability - this is to protect you from claims or lawsuits for "bodily injury" or "property damage" caused by an "occurrence."   "Occurrence" means an accident that results in bodily injury or property damage. READ THE POLICY for the other definitions.

The policy will pay up to the policy limits for damages which the insured is legally liable. The insurance company will also provide legal defense for you at their discretion. Read Chapter Six about attorneys.

Last comment about Coverage E. Make sure your policy has high liability limits. The premium for liability coverage is very inexpensive.

Lawsuits, on the other hand, are very expensive. If you can, buy the highest limits the insurance company offers. Then, seriously talk with your agent about a Liability Umbrella of at least $1 million.

Coverage F Medical Payments to Others - this is "good neighbor" insurance. If your neighbor, or the UPS driver, slips on your sidewalk and sprains her ankle, you have first dollar coverage up to a limit to pay for her medical bills. It also takes care of her if your dog bites her. Hopefully, not while she's lying on your sidewalk.

Now that you're a little more familiar with some of the things to watch for in the Homeowner policy, read the remaining chapters. They will show you the specific strategies you need to take control of your claim, and give you the utmost chance of collecting hundreds or thousands more dollars in your claim that you are already entitled to collect!!

CHAPTER ELEVEN

PROPERTY APPRAISALS AND ESTIMATES

In this chapter, we're going to look at how the value of a property claim is determined.

Before we go any further...remember this statement:

THERE IS NOTHING IN YOUR POLICY THAT REQUIRES YOU TO GET MORE THAN ONE ESTIMATE.

Many times, you'll hear an adjuster recommend that you get three estimates. That's just not necessary, and wastes your time and money. That procedure had everything to do with price, but has almost nothing to do with quality and value. Your home or your property is not a commodity...a mere rubber stamp of every other piece of property. It should not be treated like a commodity. Don't let an adjuster get away with this.

Here's another statement to remember:

AN ESTIMATE IS AN APPROXIMATE COST OF REPAIR
OR REPLACEMENT OF PROPERTY. IT IS NOT ETCHED IN
STONE. IT IS NOT A CONTRACT TO REPAIR OR REPLACE
PROPERTY.

If your loss is an automobile loss, and your vehicle is damaged, it
would be best to have your vehicle inspected by the insurance
company appraiser and your chosen body shop appraiser at the same
time. That way, they can agree on the scope of damages before they
start calculating the repair costs.

In Chapter Twenty Three, I talk about my experience recently in
an auto accident. One of the things I write about is insisting that your
body shop appraiser write an estimate using Original Equipment
Manufacturer (OEM) parts instead of aftermarket parts. Don't give in
on this point, or you'll be compromising your safety in that vehicle
after it's repaired.

In a homeowners insurance loss, in which the dwelling itself is
damaged, the claims adjuster will inspect the dwelling for damage. He
will photograph the damage and take measurements. He will make
notes of all of the damaged items, and note the quality of the building
materials. He will note the cause of the damage, if it can be readily
determined. All of that information is commonly referred to as the
"Scope of Damages."

It would be a good idea to have your contractor meet you and the
adjuster at your home at the time of the inspection. That way, you
can all look over the damage, and you, the adjuster and the contractor
can agree on the scope.

There should be an agreement between you, the policyholder, the
contractor, and the adjuster on the scope of damages. Likely, you
won't have a chance to accept the adjuster's scope until he takes the
information from his inspection back to the office and enters that
information into his estimating software in his computer. Most
adjusters will be able to print a copy of the scope and send it to you.
You should insist on a written scope of damages from the adjuster.

Don't sign anything without having your attorney review it FIRST.

Adjusters are human and sometimes miss damages. So do contractors. That's why there should be an agreement on the scope of damages...before you ever begin discussing the cost of repairs.

Think about it another way. Let's say you are going to build a new house. Your architect would have to make drawings and specifications of all of the materials that were going to be used to build that house. When it comes time to get bids from contractors, everyone bidding has the same information upon which to base their bid.

It's no different when you're getting bids and estimates in an insurance claim.

Once you have the scope of damages, you can then expect to receive the estimate from your contractor and the adjuster. The best way to handle this is to insist that the contractor and adjuster reach an agreement on the amount of the estimate. Once that's done, the adjuster can report to the insurance company and have them pay the claim.

CONTENTS, or UNSCHEDULED PERSONAL PROPERTY

Get a copy of a JC Penney catalog. Even get two...one Fall/Winter, one Spring/Summer. Get your hands on as many other catalogs as you can find. As you look at the pages of the catalogs, you'll remember the things that you had in your home. You will find hundreds or thousands of dollars in personal property that you likely would not have remembered owning. Not only will you remember dozens and dozens of items, but you'll have a retail price from a reputable retailer right at your fingertips.

Please don't misunderstand what I'm telling you to do here. I'm NOT telling you to write down items on your inventory list that you did not own. That's fraud, and you can go to jail for fraud. I'm simply showing you a way to remind yourself of things long ago purchased, and possibly stored and forgotten. For example, how many parents bought a vaporizer to run in their children's rooms at night when the children were sick? That vaporizer might not have been used in years, but you owned it, and you have a right to collect for it under the terms of your policy.

NEW INFORMATION!!

When I wrote this, I was handling a fire loss for a century-old mansion outside Atlanta that had been turned into a Bed and Breakfast. The fire was extensive, and the insurance company paid a very large amount on the dwelling alone. Then there was the contents loss which also had pretty high policy limits

This place was gorgeous, impeccably decorated and filled with antiques. I worked with the owners, a young married couple who had both worked in hospitality management for years. Now, they had an inn of their own. It appeared to me that the insurance agent did a poor job of writing adequate coverage on the property, and did not write in an endorsement for Business Income losses.

For months, the couple worked on their Contents list, trying to add everything to the list to reach the policy limits. We were already pretty confident that the loss would exceed the policy limits. However, they were just overwhelmed with this task at the same time they were managing the rebuilding of the B&B.

The insurance company claims examiner called me one Friday afternoon and told me about a company they'd been using recently. This company specialized in writing scope of damages and estimates in Contents claims. This company had some fancy software that worked great in determining the actual Contents loss. The insurance company authorized me to retain this company on behalf of the B&B owners if I deemed it necessary.

The company name is Enservio, and they can be found online at: www.enservio.com

I had a long phone conversation with the VP of Sales and Marketing, and learned about the company. Enservio serves the insurance companies, and that's who pays their fees. They specialize in Contents, whether that is business contents or personal contents.

They get paid exactly like Public Adjusters do, which is as a percentage of their total replacement/repair cost for the report they write. They refuse to work for the Public Adjusters, or represent the policyholder/claimant side of the contract.

What does that tell you?

However, in our conversation, I told the VP that I thought that an ethical Public Adjuster who wrote a very detailed inventory and appraisal performed a valuable service for the Insured. His response was that he would rather have his appraisers use certain "allowances," which translates into lump sums for classes of contents. An example would be to show an allowance for cleaning supplies, rather than actually writing down the cleaning supplies that need replacing. The insured would then have to decide whether the "allowances" were sufficient to indemnify him.

Their claim to fame and success is that they will do a very accurate inspection, and write a very accurate scope and appraisal of the damaged and destroyed personal property.

Because they are a national company, they are likely not interested into handling small losses (less than $25,000). On small losses, their service fee would probably not be high enough for the trouble. I could be wrong, though.

I can see situations in which their services would be helpful to the insurance companies. Large losses that will have extensive inventories of contents could be completed efficiently, and likely more quickly, by a contents specialty company. Also, in losses in which the Insured hires a Public Adjuster, the insurance company would then have their own expert appraisal for the Contents loss. That would be advantageous for the insurance company if a loss went to trial.

I will not either recommend them for use or warn you away from using them. Their stated goal is to write a very accurate scope and appraisal, and to hold down costs as much as possible. It seems to me that they are, in one sense, becoming the unlicensed Public Adjuster for the insurance industry.

What that means to you, the consumer, is that they have figured out a way to reduce every Contents loss more than the fee they charge the insurance company. Or else, why would an insurance company hire them to write a contents scope and appraisal? After all, the insurance company already has a staff adjuster or independent adjuster assigned to the claim who is supposed to have these skills.

Another thing that concerns me is that their appraisals must be agreed by the policyholder who had the loss. If they write an appraisal that is substantially less than the policyholder believes he is entitled to collect, what incentive would there be for the policyholder to agree to this appraisal? None that I can see.

I do see that an insurance company, faced with a disagreement between Enservio's appraisal and the Insured's appraisal (or the appraisal of the Insured's Public Adjuster), could take the position that they have a competent appraisal that they accept. Then they could issue a check to the Insured for the undisputed amount of Enservio's appraisal. That would leave the Insured to:

1. Accept the payment.
2. File a complaint with the State Department of Insurance.
3. Invoke the Appraisal Clause. (See Chapter Twenty)
4. File suit against the insurance company.

Just remember, you can't hire these people to represent you. The insurance company will have to agree to hire them and pay their fee. My recommendation is to refuse to sign any document in which you agree to accept Enservio's appraisal for your Contents claim as a condition for hiring them on your behalf.

Our Bed and Breakfast owners didn't need the help of the

contents specialist company. They carefully documented all of their personal property, and we settled their claim.

CHAPTER TWELVE

ADDITIONAL LIVING EXPENSE CLAIMS

In a Homeowner insurance policy, you'll usually see this coverage listed as Coverage D. Sometimes, it's called Loss of Use.

Additional Living Expense (ALE) coverage is just what you might think it is. When you have a covered loss that makes the place you reside unfit to live in, and it forces you to spend more on normal operating costs than you usually spend, ALE coverage pays.

Your policy probably reads just like the following: "Additional Living Expense, meaning any necessary increases in living expenses incurred by you so that your household can maintain its normal standard of living."

ALE covers things like:

a. Temporary housing, like in a hotel or apartment. Remember, if you had a mortgage on your home, you still have to pay the mortgage payment while the home is being repaired. Lots of times the loss is severe and the adjuster knows you'll be out of your home for weeks or months. The insurance company will save money if it places your family in an extended stay hotel, or in a short term apartment lease. In addition to saving money on rent, the insurance company can pay advances on Contents, and if you're in an apartment, you'll have a place to store your new contents, like furniture, clothing and kitchenware.

b. Laundry and dry cleaning. If you had laundry facilities at your residence, it will cost you more to get your clothes cleaned. The extra cost you incur is covered.

c. Meals. This is where many people misunderstand their claim. Certainly, if you cannot buy and prepare your own meals, you'll incur higher food prices. But insurance companies won't usually pay for costly steak dinners and high bar tabs. You're going to have to be able to explain your meal purchases, so don't go overboard. You'll have to make an accurate estimate of what your family normally spends per month on food. That can certainly include restaurant meals that you normally buy. Just remember that ALE is paying for items OVER your normal standard of living. Keep METICULOUS RECORDS of your food purchases. If the insurance company places you into a temporary apartment or efficiency hotel that has a kitchen, they'll stop paying for most extra meals.

d. Boarding costs for pets. Someone has to take care of your pets while you cannot live in your home. This is covered.

e. Increased transportation costs for all your vehicles. Do you have to drive your children to school, since your temporary accommodations are not in the old school district? That's covered. Do you have to drive further to and from work? Covered. Do you have further to drive to doctors, dentists, ballet classes, soccer games, etc.? The increased cost is covered. Did I say KEEP METICULOUS RECORDS? Most office supply stores have automobile expense logbooks for sale for a dollar or two. Stop by and pick up one for each car you drive, and write down EVERY TRIP. Keep all receipts for every penny you spend on transportation.

f. Furniture rental for a temporary residence. You have to have chairs and beds and other stuff...even pots and pans, dishes and temporary electronics. However, don't try to get them to pay for a 60" plasma flat screen TV rental if you had a 27" color TV at home.

g. Relocation and storage expenses. Perhaps some of your personal property was not damaged. Perhaps some was damaged, but the restoration contractor is cleaning and repairing it. Once it's cleaned and repaired, it's got to be stored somewhere until you can move back home. Covered.

h. Costs of telephone or utility installation at your temporary residence. This would include deposits that the utility companies might require. Don't forget garbage pickup at your temporary place. It's all covered. Even cable TV hookups would be covered if you had cable at home prior to the loss.

What if you stayed with relatives, and did not incur increased rent, and many of the other expenses shown above? Another scenario is that you just simply do not want to go through the process of documenting all of your extra expenses. The policy gives you the option to be paid "Fair Rental Value", which is: "the fair rental value of that part of the 'residence premises' where you reside less any expenses that do not continue while the premises is not fit to live in."

How much would your house rent for? That's the question.

You'll need to make a comparison between your residence, like it was before the loss, and properties in the neighborhood that are comparable to yours. A good real estate broker can be very helpful in substantiating these comparable properties and the monthly costs of them. Once you determine the Fair Rental Value of your home, you must subtract expenses that do not continue during the restoration period, such as some utilities, garbage pickup, landscaping services or maid services.

Some insurance companies will still pay for extra transportation costs, relocation expenses, storage of contents and utilities in addition to Fair Rental Value. Some will make you choose either ALE or Fair Rental Value. Find out from your insurance company what they are going to do, and make your decision.

Go to the website at: www.insurance-claim-secrets.com and find the Resources tab. Download the ALE worksheet and make as many copies as you need. Use it as your guide to record and submit your ALE claim.

If your records and receipts were damaged in your loss, contact your utility companies, credit card companies and other creditors and get copies of the last couple months' bills. You'll need these records to confirm your normal operating expenses.

Finally: Don't be surprised if your adjuster or claims examiner tries to disqualify some of your legitimate expenses. Don't just accept what the adjuster says. If it's a truly legitimate expense, <u>FIGHT FOR IT</u>!! Go over the adjuster's head to his supervisor. <u>Keep fighting</u>. Send them a letter that insists that they give you written denial of any legitimate expenses. Once you have that in your possession, call your state Department of Insurance (DOI) and register a written complaint. You never know what impact a DOI complaint will have on your claim.

CHAPTER THIRTEEN

THREE DEAD IN ALCOHOL RELATED TRAFFIC MISHAP, NO ONE DRINKING

Or, "Beer kills three motorists, but no one drank a drop."

One of the crazy reasons that I love the claims business is that it provides me with the most bizarre stories. Here is the most bizarre claim I handled in 2005, perhaps the most bizarre ever.

I received this claim from an insurer in London. They insured an engineering company in Florida that did soils testing for a bridge building project. There were two bridges crossing a river, and the State of Florida and Brevard County were rebuilding both bridges.

The roadway on either side of the bridge had two lanes northbound and two lanes southbound, separated by a grass median. There was a construction zone about a quarter mile long through the bridge project. Traffic from the southbound lanes was diverted to one lane of the northbound bridge. The posted speed limit in the construction zone was 35 miles per hour. There were all of the barriers, and orange cones, and signage that you'd expect in a construction zone.

Our insured, the engineering company, was a co-defendant in the Wrongful Death lawsuit filed by the families of the three people that died in an accident that happened in the construction zone. The Plaintiffs sued the State, the County, the General Contractor, all of the subcontractors, and the retailer who sold the beer in question. Plaintiffs asserted that the construction zone was designed improperly, and caused the horrific wreck.

Here's what really happened.

Back in 2001, in a four-door '87 Honda Civic was a 15 year old girl, a 16 year old girl, a 17 year old girl and a 25 year old adult male. They had left a beach party near Cocoa Beach and headed to the local beer retailer, where it was their task to buy a full keg of beer and bring it back to the party. On the way from the beach to the store, the 17 year old girl was driving.

They arrived at the store, and the 25 year old male bought the keg. A store employee wheeled the keg out to the car on a handcart, and they placed the keg on its side in the trunk of the Honda Civic. (The store had this on tape from their security camera) They did not secure the keg from rolling around in the trunk. The full keg weighed 140 pounds.

At this point, the three passengers and driver discussed that they needed to get back to the party fast. The 17 year old girl refused to drive any faster on the way back. So, the 16 year old girl volunteered to drive faster on the way back to the beach.

The 16 year old, driving about 60 miles per hour, entered the construction zone driving southbound. Just as she neared the south end of the zone, she lost control of the car. The car went sideways, slid through the grass median, and entered the left active lane of northbound traffic. The Civic was struck right behind the driver's door by a northbound auto. The impact was so strong that it cut the Honda in half. The two people in the rear seats…the 15 year old girl and the 25 year old male, died instantly. The force of the impact spun the severed rear of the Civic, and this centrifugal force caused the trunk to pop open.

The 140-pound keg of beer was sent airborne. It went through the windshield of the next northbound auto, a Saturn four door sedan. The keg landed on the driver, killing him instantly. The driver was a 28 year old male adult, with his mother in the front passenger seat, and a male friend in the right rear passenger seat. The mother was seriously injured, but lived. They were on their way to have dinner at Red Lobster.

No one in either vehicle had drunk a drop of alcohol, yet three died because of a keg of beer.

The 16-year old driver pled guilty to a Vehicular Homicide charge, and spent a little over a year in Juvenile Detention until she turned 18.

The insurance company hired a local attorney to defend the engineering company. We negotiated a settlement with the Plaintiff's attorney. We had a very strong case and were prepared to go to trial to defend our client. However, in order to make the lawsuit go away for our client, we offered the Plaintiff's attorney the amount of money we estimated that it would take for Defense counsel to try the case in court. The Plaintiffs accepted the money, signed a Full Release and dropped our client out of the lawsuit.

I tell this story often because it's so weird, and because it actually happened.

What lessons can be learned from this? How about these?

1. Teenaged drivers do stupid things, and that's the reason they have such high car insurance premiums.

2. Boy drivers are the stupidest, but even girl drivers can be stupid.

3. The company you keep can cost you your life.

4. However sometimes death is so random you cannot plan to prevent it.

5. You should carry very high liability limits on your auto insurance policy. Why? Because plaintiffs usually sue everybody involved in an auto accident. Even though you may not have caused the accident, you could have your life ruined by a lawsuit. Your auto insurance company owes you a defense under your liability coverage, but only up to the policy limits. If you have minimal coverage, just enough to be legal, that's all the insurance company will owe. What would you do if your policy limits were $50,000, and a jury awarded the Plaintiff $300,000? Or a million?

6. Buy a Liability Umbrella policy with limits of at least one million dollars. Two million would be better. The policy is cheap coverage.

CHAPTER FOURTEEN

HURRICANE LOSSES

Thirteen major hurricanes have hit the coastal US since summer of 2004. They are named:

Charlie - landfall in Florida, Category 4
Gaston - landfall in South Carolina, Category 1
Frances - landfall in Florida and Alabama, Category 3
Ivan - landfall in Alabama, Category 3
Jeanne - landfall in Florida, Category 3
Dennis - landfall in Florida, Category 4
Katrina - landfall in FL, AL, MS, and LA,   Category 4
Rita - landfall in Louisiana and Texas, Category 4
Wilma - landfall in Florida, Category 4
Dolly, Fay, Gustav, and Ike, Gulf Coast in 2008

These thirteen hurricanes caused damages far in excess of $250 billion dollars.

Climatologists at the National Climactic Data Center (www.ncdc.noaa.gov) and the Department of Atmospheric Science at Colorado State University say that they expect the next few years to be equally severe as 2004 and 2005.

Filing a claim after a hurricane has its own little quirks, but the process is pretty much the same as any other claim filing. If you follow the directions in this book, you'll probably come out far better than your neighbors who haven't read this book. But, don't be an un-neighborly neighbor. Tell them the website address so they can get one of their own. Or, tell them to go to their favorite bookstore and pick up a copy.

When a hurricane strikes where you live, here is what you should do to protect your property and protect your insurance claim.

AFTER THE STORM

1. When you can safely get to your property, inspect the property and find out what needs to be done.

2. Take a camera, lots of film (or disposable cameras) and a pad of paper. Photograph ALL DAMAGE, INTERIOR AND EXTERIOR. TAKE PHOTOS OF CONTENTS DAMAGE. There might be hidden damage…don't worry about that. Just get photos of the damage in plain sight. Don't wait for the adjuster to do this. He might be days or weeks from inspecting your property. Your insurance contract requires you to mitigate your damage.

3. Describe in writing on your pad of paper all of the damage you can see.

4. ONLY THEN should you think about mitigating your damage. Remember, the word "mitigate" is an insurance term that means protecting the property from further damage. This can be placing tarps over damaged roofing, or pumping water out of your home or other temporary repairs. The costs for temporary repairs to protect your property are covered in your policy.

5. GET YOUR POLICY AND READ IT. Notify your insurance company that you have a claim. See Chapter Four, "Notify Your Insurance Company."

6. DON'T THROW ANYTHING AWAY QUITE YET. If you're making a pile of debris, make sure you photograph and write down everything that goes into the pile.

7. CALL A PUBLIC ADJUSTING COMPANY AND HAVE THEM EVALUATE YOUR LOSS. See Chapter Nine.

8. CALL AN ATTORNEY WHO KNOWS INSURANCE CLAIMS LAW. See Chapter Six, "Should I Get a Lawyer?"

Let me give you a few basic guidelines about claims after a hurricane.

You should realize right now that thousands of other people have damaged property, and insurance company response is going to take some time.

Having said that, please remember that the old saying "A squeaky wheel gets the grease" is even more true in a catastrophe situation. Claims adjusters and company claims examiners are human, and they don't like to be annoyed any more than you do. If you are constantly, relentlessly, politely demanding, they will place your claim at the top of their list. They will want to get rid of you, and the way to do that is to get your claim paid.

I promise you that most of the people filing a claim will patiently wait like sheep waiting to be shorn. <u>If you will do what this book says, you'll get more money and get it sooner.</u>

Also, if you retain a Public Adjusting company, they will expedite your claim, and characteristically help you collect far more money.

You should realize right now that insurance companies send adjusters and temporary adjusters called "Storm Troopers" to your area to help with the overflow of claims.

Storm Troopers are people who are trying to do a good job as adjusters. However, in many cases, they are only trained for a few days or a couple weeks before being sent to your area. So, when the adjuster arrives at your property ask him if he is a temporary adjuster. If he is, you know up front that you may have a potential problem with the scope of your damages, and the amount of the estimate.

Remember that the estimate that any adjuster writes for your damages IS ONLY AN ESTIMATE. IT IS NOT A CONTRACT

TO REPAIR YOUR PROPERTY. The chances are overwhelming that you will not be able to find a contractor to repair your property for the amount of the estimate. This is because materials and labor prices increase after a storm because of supply and demand. I don't know of any estimating software used by adjusters that takes into account the rapid increase in repair costs in an area that has suffered a catastrophe.

Remember that nowhere in your policy does it say that you have to get two or three estimates for repairs. Get the contractor of your choice, not the choice of the insurance company. If you agree to use the insurance company's approved contractor, that's your decision. Finding contractors in the wake of a hurricane is sometimes a real challenge.

Most insurance companies want a preliminary estimate so that they can set their reserves. This is important for the insurance company because they have to set aside money to pay claims, and they want the amounts they set aside to be as accurate as possible. If they set aside too little money, the insurance regulators for each state get mad at them. If they set aside to much money, that adversely affects their investment income.

Most insurance companies also want to pay claims as soon as possible. So, if they get a preliminary estimate from the adjuster, they can issue an initial payment to their policyholder. That helps you, the policyholder, begin repairs sooner. Most people don't have tens of thousands of dollars just sitting around that they can use to hire contractors to repair their property, and then wait for the insurance company to reimburse them. Most contractors need money up front to begin repairs, as they have to buy materials before they begin repairs. They need the insurance payment to be made quickly to get the process started.

The best possible scenario for getting your claim paid more quickly is to have the adjuster and your contractor meet at your property and inspect it together. That way, they can agree on the scope of the damages right then. Later, when they both write an estimate, they can negotiate an agreed estimate based on their earlier agreement on the scope. You won't believe how much time this cuts out of your claim if it works.

Let me tell you about claims adjusters after Katrina and Rita. I was working as a Claims Supervisor. I did a few really large losses in New Orleans, but then my employer needed me to help with supervision. The field adjusters sent their reports to us in the home office, and we made sure they were accurate before sending them along to the Claims Departments at various insurance companies.

The field adjusters working out of the Catastrophe Offices down at the Gulf Shores area got assigned hundreds of claims each. There are only so many hours in a day, so frustration can set in very quickly for field adjusters.

First, they have to drive to the loss location. Many times the street signs and road signs have been blown away, so just finding the location is a challenge. When I worked Hurricane Andrew in Miami in 1992, we had to take detailed street maps and just count streets to find a house. All of the signs were gone.

Next, they have to try to meet the insured at the location. Many times, the homeowners were not there when the adjuster arrived…either they had evacuated to another town or state, or just had trouble getting back home.

Next, they have to inspect the property. Hopefully, it's not raining. Hopefully, the roof is not too high for the ladder they carry with them. Hopefully, the roof is not too steep to walk on. Hopefully, the owner doesn't have a mean dog.

Next comes the photos. Let me tell you how hard it is to keep photos straight when you're inspecting ten houses a day, six days a week.

It's real hard. Really, reeeeeealy hard.

Next, you have to make a diagram of the building and take really good notes on the damage.

Now, sometime you have to stop inspecting buildings and go back to your motel room and start writing estimates.

Unfortunately, some adjusters will inspect dozens of properties before they begin writing estimates. It's nearly impossible to remember a house you looked at a month ago and try to write an accurate estimate. Most of the time, it's a challenge to remember what you did two days ago.

But the other way of doing it...inspect a few, write the estimate and report, inspect a few more...is just as time consuming as the other way. This is why some policyholders had to wait weeks and months before they could get an adjuster just to inspect the house.

So, even though it's terrible to have to wait weeks or months for your claim to be paid, there actually is a logical reason why the process takes so long in the aftermath of a major hurricane.

Turn in the book to Chapter Four, "Don't be in a Hurry." Do what it says.

Read Chapter Twenty Two, "Mold Claims."

CHAPTER FIFTEEN

THANKS, I DEPRECIATE THAT

OK...I know that's a malapropism, but forgive me. I'm trying to make this book somewhat entertaining while teaching you how to collect hundreds or thousands of dollars in insurance proceeds that you're entitled to collect.

I'm an insurance adjuster, not Rodney Dangerfield!

Nearly every insurance policy that covers some kind of property...homes, contents, automobiles, commercial businesses, trucks and their cargo, ships and their cargo...deals with the valuation of the insured property.

Most property coverage starts out by insuring property for its ACTUAL CASH VALUE, or ACV. Permit me a few moments to explain what ACV is.

We'll start with the other concept in property valuation, and that is REPLACEMENT COST VALUATION, or RCV. That simply means the cost to replace any item that is insured. For example, you have a 2000 Toyota Celica and you paid $20,000 for it. If the car got in an accident and the damage was a total loss, it might cost you $22,000 to buy a 2005 Toyota Celica exactly like the damaged car. So, $22,000 would be your Replacement Cost.

It works just like that on any item of property. It also works kind of in reverse on items like electronics. If you bought a laptop for $1,500 in 2002, chances are that the same laptop in 2006 costs $999.00 or less. But, that's still the RCV.

Actual Cash Value (ACV) is the depreciated value of any property.

Let's try to understand the word "Depreciation" as it relates to insurance.

Every article of property has a useful life. For example, your washing machine may have a useful life of ten years. If the washing machine was worth 100% of its value when you bought it, and it has a useful life of ten years, then it loses 10% of its value each year. By the tenth year, it has an ACV of $0. That doesn't mean that you should throw it away. That doesn't mean it doesn't still work great. We're only talking about ACV.

Depreciation is affected by more than just age. Wear and tear are big important factors in determining depreciation. If that washing machine has a ten year useful life, that's under perfect conditions. But if it get used hard, and not maintained well, that will shorten its useful life.

Think about the useful life of what goes into that washer…your clothes. Clothing has a short useful life. That nice pair of slacks you bought might only have a useful life of 2 or 3 years. If it were 2 years, then the slacks would depreciate 50% per year. At 3 years, the slacks would depreciate 33% per year. Children's clothes can get worn out in 3 months.

In insurance, an insurance company or adjuster will determine the Replacement Cost Value of an item of property...the RCV. Then, he will factor in the useful life and the condition of the property at the time of the loss...that's the depreciation. He'll subtract the depreciation from the RCV, and the sum remaining is the ACV...the Actual Cash Value.

OK...do you understand the concept of Depreciation, RCV and ACV now?

Let me give you the best two examples of ACV I know.

1. Go to a garage sale, and buy something used. What you paid for that item that day is its truest ACV.
2. Go to the wonderful auction site Ebay. Look at the prices sellers are getting for selling something used at auction. Those prices for that item that day are its truest ACV.

Let me explain to you why this is important in EVERY PROPERTY INSURANCE CLAIM.

You are going to get paid based upon the valuation of your property by an adjuster and the insurance company who insures your property.

Even in a liability claim, the same thing happens with adjusters and insurers. If your vehicle is struck by another vehicle, and the accident is his fault, and your car is a total loss...the other guy's insurance company is going to try to depreciate your car in the settlement.

But, it's not just the "other guy's" insurance that's going to try to take advantage of you.

Your own insurance company is going to try to "lowball" you, or get you to accept the lowest possible amount of money in settlement.

Next are the most important two questions that exist concerning depreciation:

ARE YOU READY??

HERE THEY COME!!!

1. Who determines the correct amount of depreciation?
2. What method is used in determining depreciation?

Answer to Question 1:

The insurance company will determine the amount of depreciation that is subtracted from the replacement cost of your property UNLESS YOU CHALLENGE THEIR FIGURES.

Answer to Question 2:

A. Insurance companies and insurance adjusters use published depreciation tables to determine the useful life and depreciation of a vast assortment of property. I have posted depreciation tables in the Resources Section on my website that you can print off for yourself. I've also listed links that you can click on to see other depreciation tables.

B. Most adjusters and claims departments these days have sophisticated estimating software that has the depreciation tables built right into it. So, when the adjuster writes his estimate, he will enter certain data, like the age and condition of the property, and the estimating program automatically depreciates the property.

C. Lots of times, an adjuster will use his experience and just take a wild guess. This is sometimes known as "Gut Depreciation". It's a wild guess based on past experience in calculating claims. You might have heard this sort of guessing called a WAG (wild-a** guess) or a SWAG (scientific wild-a** guess) or an EWAG (educated wild a** guess). You would be very surprised how often a WAG, EWAG or SWAG is used in an insurance adjuster's life. You'd also likely be surprised how often adjusters' WAGs are accurate.

But now, let's consider how this depreciation, RCV, and ACV stuff affects YOU in your claims.

A standard Homeowner's Policy settles the Dwelling loss on RCV. However, it settles the Contents loss (sometimes referred to as Unscheduled Personal Property, or UPP) on ACV. Read your policy carefully to determine what kind of coverage you have.

Most insurance companies have an endorsement that you can buy that provides replacement cost valuation on your Contents. The premium is only a few dollars more, and you should NEVER be without this endorsement on your policy. If you find that you do not have this Replacement Cost (RC) coverage on your Contents, DO NOT LET ANOTHER 24 HOURS PASS BEFORE YOU ADD IT TO YOUR POLICY.

So, if you have a Homeowners loss, and you don't have the RC endorsement, the adjuster is going to depreciate ALL of your contents. ALL OF THEM.

If you have a policy that has the Replacement Cost Valuation endorsement for Contents, the adjuster and insurance company is going to use depreciation to create something called a "holdback of recoverable depreciation."

Remember Chapter One, "Water, Water Everywhere?" In that chapter, I told you about recoverable depreciation. My homeowners insurance company used this process in my water claim. They will use the same process in your Contents claim.

Our Homeowner Policy had a Replacement Cost Value (RCV) clause. Here's what the policy says about RCV at the time of a loss:

"Conditions, How losses are settled.

2. Under Unscheduled Personal Property Coverages:

We will pay only the actual cash value of the damaged property until actual repair or replacement is completed."

So, even if you have the RC Endorsement on your policy, the insurance company will hold back the recoverable depreciation until you replace your damaged property. If the adjuster doesn't calculate depreciation correctly, the insurance company could withhold hundreds or thousands of dollars from you that you need to replace your damaged property.

Remember the reason I wrote this book? To show you how to collect hundreds or thousands of dollars MORE in settlement that you are entitled to collect?

Well, you are entitled to a VERY ACCURATE calculation of your CONTENTS loss.

Here are the things that YOU MUST DO.

1. Go to the website at: http://www.insurance-claim-secrets.com Click on the Resources tab. Find the Contents Inventory form. Print a form and make as many copies as you need. This is what you're going to submit to the adjuster or insurance company to document your loss.

2. List everything that has been damaged...down to the last thumbtack, extra pair of shoe laces and bobby pin. Hey...you paid for this stuff. If it got damaged in a covered loss, the insurance company is bound by their contract with you to make you whole again. There is NOTHING that you own that is too small or insignificant to be listed on your Contents Inventory form.

3. List the age of every item to the best of your ability. In a fire or tornado or hurricane loss, there could be hundreds of items that you don't have receipts for. But that doesn't mean they didn't exist. List them.

Here's a terrific tip. Pictures are worth a thousand words. Go to your local JC Penney store and get a copy of the latest catalog, either

Spring/Summer or Fall/Winter. Better yet, see if you can get both double season catalogs. Get other specialty catalogs if necessary. Then take the inventory list and start thumbing through the pages. You'll be amazed at the things you'll remember owning that should be on your inventory list. Not only will the catalogs stimulate your memory, but give you the latest price of that item right in front of you. Sure, some of your stuff may be of higher quality than Penney's, but if you're in a hot negotiation with the insurance company over the value of your contents, you're assured that you should get at LEAST the value found in the catalog.

4. Produce as many receipts and invoices as you possibly can to prove that you owned your contents. Receipts will also prove the age of the items automatically.

5. Remember in Chapter Four, when I told you to photograph or take video footage of every room, every closet, every drawer in your home, and put that tape in your safe deposit box or some other secure offsite storage? Now is the time to get that tape and look it over. The insurance company may want a copy of the tape. Give them a copy if they ask, but only if they ask. Don't EVER give them your original tape.

6. Require the adjuster or the insurance company to provide you with a copy or copies of the exact depreciation tables that they used to determine the depreciation on every item of your Inventory list. Once you have the tables, you can compare each item to the tables to make sure that you are paid exactly what each item is worth.

7. What if you find that your adjuster or insurance company has used the WAG/SWAG method? DO NOT ACCEPT IT. There are depreciation tables for nearly everything. Insist on receiving the depreciation tables that the adjuster or insurance company used on your claim.

You need to have access to depreciation tables that are industry accepted tables. So, here's another resource for anyone with a computer and the ability to go to a website.

Go to: http://www.claimspages.com

At the top of the homepage is a blue horizontal bar that has words in it. Move your cursor to the right until it is over the word "Tools." Click on it. Move your cursor down to "Depreciation Calculator." Click on it.

Now, a page will open that allows you to find a depreciation schedule either by keyword search, or on another drop down menu that lists every type of property from different categories.

This is a SUPER tool! This tool will get you hundreds…possibly thousands of dollars more in your Contents claim, because the depreciation will be accurately calculated.

Once you prove that you've replaced the damaged property, the insurance company will release the holdback amount to you.

You see, it's simple…but not easy!

CHAPTER SIXTEEN

RESIDENTIAL WATER CLAIMS

Water....we can't live without it.

The planet is mostly water. Our bodies are about 90% water. If water doesn't fall from the sky in certain places, we call those places deserts. If a lot of water falls from the sky on certain places, we call them floods...or jungles.

Not enough water can kill you. Too much water can kill you, too.

It was a great event when someone first put a water well and a hand pump inside a dwelling. No more carrying water from the outside well. But, the more technologically advanced our water systems have become, the more ways there are to have water damage our homes.

A good rule of thumb about water damage is this phrase: "If the water comes down, it might be covered. If the water comes up, it is probably not covered."

Look at just some of the ways water can damage a home:
-Roof leak
-Drain pipe under the kitchen sink leaks
-Icemaker water supply line leaks
-Air conditioner condensation drain line clogs and overflows
-Toilet overflows
-Tub overflows
-Washing machine drain pipe bursts
-Washing machine water supply line leaks
-Dishwasher water supply leaks
-Dishwasher drain leaks
-Water seeps through the basement wall
-Sewer backup
-Sump pump fails
-Shower pan leaks
-Water line in an outside wall freezes in winter
-Flood from river, lake or stream nearby
-Tidal surge in a coastal hurricane
-Fire happens, fire department hoses down your house or apartment with water
-Fire happens in the apartment above you, and the fire department hoses down the fire, and the water leaks into your apartment.

Some of these examples of water damage are covered by insurance, and others are not. It depends on the terms of your policy, and it also depends on the cause of the water damage.

A good example to lead off with is a roof leak. Many times, the policy requires there to be a covered peril that caused the leak. That would be something like wind, hail or falling objects like tree limbs. If there is no covered peril, many times the interior damage will not be covered.

So, you could have water stains on ceilings, or even worse water damage, and not have coverage because the policy does not cover it. Flashing around chimneys, around vent pipes and around attic vents wears out and allows leaks. In addition, shingle nails pop up and shingles wear out. These are the types of conditions that most policies will not cover.

Sometimes, the policy will cover water damage to the interior, such as ceiling damage, but won't repair the roof leak. Read your policy.

Water damage claims are probably the most common of all homeowner claims. Still, you may have a challenge getting your water damage claim paid by the insurance company.

Let's talk first about the biggest water claim, which is a flood. Usually, a flood will cause huge damage to your dwelling, and make it uninhabitable for a time. Everything gets wet, and the water in a flood is usually very contaminated with soil, mud, chemicals and even raw sewage.

The flood loss is also the loss that is most misunderstood. That's because most flood damage is excluded from most insurance policies. Usually, a person must purchase a separate Flood policy, either from an insurance company or through the Federal Government's National Flood Insurance Program.

Sometimes, you have to qualify for flood insurance by living in a designated flood plain. However, that did not matter during the hurricane season of 2004 in Florida, and the Gulf Coast in 2005. There were thousands of homeowners that had their homes damaged by floodwaters that lived nowhere near designated flood plains. The insurance companies denied thousands of claims because the damage was not covered under their normal insurance policies.

The Florida Legislature tried to make the insurance companies pay for flood claims in policies where floods were not covered, but were not successful.

In 2006, a Louisiana court found in favor of Nationwide Insurance Company when they were sued by one of their insureds for denying a claim. The Court found that insurance companies CAN deny claims for wind-driven flood water.

Let's talk about what YOU should do when you have a water loss, no matter what size it is.

THE MOST IMPORTANT THING TO REMEMBER IS...

SPEED!

There's a word in the insurance claims business, and that word is "mitigate," or "mitigation." The dictionary defines it as "to moderate in force or intensity." In insurance claims, it simply means to make the damage less, or to stop the damage from getting worse.

The faster you can begin repairs on water damage, the less damage there will be.

Restoration contractors are tremendous assets in water damage claims. Most of us don't know how to clean up water and prevent the water from doing more damage. Most of us don't own the equipment necessary to repair water damage and dry out the wet areas. Restoration contractors do.

Often the restoration contractor is the first one to begin the process of cleanup. Lots of times, the adjuster himself will call in a contractor to do emergency work. They may set up big fans or dehumidifiers. They may pull up all the carpet and the pad. They may even remove some of the baseboards and drywall.

Let's talk about carpet and vinyl flooring for a minute or two.

What if you've bought an expensive carpet for your home, and the adjuster just thinks it's a builder grade carpet?

Who's going to win? <u>You will, if you prove your case.</u>

There is a way that you can be sure that you receive the exact amount that you should receive to replace your damaged carpet or vinyl. Even if you have replacement cost coverage in your policy, you must know the quality and price of the original to determine the replacement cost.

The most obvious way is to produce the receipt for the carpet you bought. But, what if you don't have the receipt anymore, or it was installed years ago by the builder? What if the receipt got burned in the fire? What if you just bought the house and have no idea about the age, make and model of the carpet?

There is a testing laboratory named ITEL Labs in Jacksonville, Florida. They have become one of the world's most knowledgeable authorities on flooring. They have tens of thousands of samples of carpet and vinyl from the flooring manufacturers. For less than $40, they will send you a packet with a self addressed return envelope and other bags. You'll cut out a small piece of vinyl or carpet and pad, and send it back to them.

The laboratory will send you a report, telling you the manufacturer, model or design, information about the carpet fiber and the type of backing, and the price of the carpet.

They will do the same for vinyl flooring.

Here's ITEL's contact information:

ITEL Laboratories (Independent Testing Evaluation Laboratories)
6747 Phillips Industrial Blvd, Suite 1
Jacksonville, FL 32256
904-363-0196
Fax 904-363-2379
Website: www.itelinc.com

If your floor covering is worth hundreds or thousands to replace, it will be worth $40 to prove the true cost of your carpet or vinyl flooring.

By the way…the insurance company should pay for the testing of the flooring as a cost of adjusting the claim. However, if they refuse, it's still in your best interest to bear the small cost yourself.

Carpet can be saved in most cases if it gets wet, even soaking wet with clean water. It usually cannot be saved in a muddy flood. The pad underneath the carpet is foam of some sort, and holds water like a sponge. It's very normal for the restoration contractor to pull up the carpet and pad, and dispose of the pad right away.

The backing on carpet will delaminate if it stays wet for too long, and once that happens, the carpet must be thrown out.

Most of the nasty odor associated with wet carpet is found in the pad, not the carpet. Even when you have problems with pet urine, the urine has soaked into the pad, not the carpet. Get rid of the pad, usually that gets rid of the odor.

Sometimes, the carpet can be dried out without removing it from the dwelling. When the damage is more serious, the contractor may take the carpet to his facility for drying and cleaning.

Replacing damaged carpet is a hotly contested topic in many, many claims. Most of the time, the claims adjuster simply guesses at the age, quality and price of your carpet. Most of the time, he gets it wrong. Most of the time, his guess on the price is far too low.

Another important thing to do is to get the furniture off the wet carpet as soon as possible. Furniture with legs very often has a metal "shoe" or skid plate at the bottom of the leg. If that metal shoe sits too long on the wet carpet, it could rust, and cause a stain that cannot be removed. Lots of times, the restoration contractor will put the furniture up on wood or plastic blocks. Getting the furniture off the wet carpet also prevents the furniture from absorbing the water and becoming damaged.

Remember the word, "SPEED?"

It's super important if you have wood floors. Wood floors swell and buckle if they get too much water on them for too long a period of time. Many times, wood floors can be saved from damage if the water is removed quickly. Get a restoration contactor to get the water off the floor. Contractors know how to dry out the floor and save it, and that can save thousands in repairs.

Another common source of water damage is water that leaks from a plumbing, heating, air conditioning system or appliance. Many policies will pay for the damage that the water causes, but will not pay to repair the source. For example, if you have a shower pan that leaks, the policy may pay to access the drain so that it can be fixed, but won't pay to repair the drain. The same would be true for a water supply line or drain line is in or under a concrete slab. The policy will likely pay to access the drain or pipe, but would not pay for the repair of the pipe or drain.

Homeowner policies vary as it relates to water that backs up into the house from drains. Most of the time, if you have a clogged drain that backs up within the four walls of the dwelling, the damage is covered. If the sewer outside the four walls backs up into your home, it might not be covered. READ YOUR POLICY!

Water claims require you to do the same things that any other loss requires of you, which are:

Know what's in your policy.
Keep good documentation and records.
Fight for every dollar of coverage you have.

CHAPTER SEVENTEEN

DEDUCT THIS!

In most insurance policies, there is a deductible. This is, in essence, your "self insurance" contribution to any loss.

Few policies anymore have a zero deductible, although you can still find them.

The higher your deductible, the lower your premium. The insurance company rewards you for accepting a larger amount of losses.

If you have the financial ability, it's always better to accept a higher deductible. You'll usually save a bunch of premium dollars, since you don't have losses very often.

You can find out more about managing your deductibles at the website and in our monthly newsletter. Go to the website to find out.

Let's talk about the deductible you have in your policy right now.

There are a couple ways that deductibles can be handled. For example, if you have an automobile collision or comprehensive loss, you can pay your deductible to the body shop or the glass shop. Then, the insurance company will pay the remaining amount of the claim.

In a Contents claim, the customary method of settlement is to subtract the deductible from the total, and pay the claim. Then, when you begin replacing your property, you have to use your own money equal to the deductible.

In a Homeowners claim, if there is a contractor or cleaning vendor involved, you'd pay your deductible to the vendor, and then the insurance company will pay the remaining amount of the claim.

Traditionally, in an insurance policy, there is one deductible assessed for each OCCURRENCE. For example, when a tornado hits your home, it damages the house, the outbuildings, the contents, and you have to move somewhere else temporarily. Four separate coverages are affected, but it occurred once. One deductible is assessed.

In some policies, such as commercial property policies, in which there are multiple locations or multiple buildings on one location, you might find that the policy requires a deductible be assessed for each LOCATION or BUILDING.

After the large number of hurricanes that happened over the last few years in the USA, the insurance companies changed deductibles in locations that were more likely to be struck by a hurricane. In those areas, they usually did one of two things:

1. Added a Wind and Hail Exclusion endorsement to the policy. If you have that endorsement, you likely have NO coverage for wind or hail. Check your policy to see if you have that new endorsement.
2. Changed the deductible to a percentage of the loss. Customary percentages found are 2%, 3%, or 5% of the amount of COVERAGE. For example, if you had a policy with $100,000 coverage on your dwelling, and a 5% wind/hail deductible, your

deductible amount is $5,000. Read your policy to determine what your deductible is.

Sometimes a loss is so large that it exceeds the policy limits. For example, your policy insures your home for $100,000.00. The house burns to the ground, and the estimate to rebuild the house is $110,000.00. You have a $1,000 deductible in your policy. In this example, you would not be assessed a deductible. The insurance company figures that your actual loss is greater than your policy limits plus your deductible. So, your deductible is absorbed by the amount of your loss that is greater than the limits.

That's about all I can say about deductibles. My newsletter will offer tips on managing the deductibles on all of your insurance policies to maximize your coverages and minimize your premiums. Plus I'll send newsletters about all kinds of great information to help you. Sign up for the free monthly newsletter at the website.

CHAPTER EIGHTEEN

DISC-CATCHING DOG

I've changed the names in this story to protect the confidentiality of the claimant.

I got called out in the wee hours of the morning on a trucking liability claim assignment a few years ago. According to the file information, a young man named Jeremy, driving a small pickup truck, flipped his truck and was injured, and our trucker was somehow to blame. I got the assignment less than an hour after the mishap occurred.

On I-75 northbound going out of Atlanta, there is an exit and entrance to the highway at Wade Green Road. The entrance ramp from Wade Green onto northbound I-75 is quite long. On the left and right of the active lanes are emergency lanes. Eighteen wheeler drivers like to park on this entrance ramp on each side of the active lanes and sleep. Every 100 feet on the entire entrance ramp is a big "No Parking" sign in white and red. They're impossible to miss. Unfortunately, the local police don't enforce this law much, since nearly anytime you drive by that ramp, there's at least one big rig parked in there.

Seems our truck driver pulled into the right side emergency lane and parked the big rig, but left his back end out in the active lane a little. Sometime around 4:00 am, Jeremy came down the ramp in his pickup truck, and it was foggy at the time. He came up on the rear of the trailer in the fog, and swerved left to avoid striking the trailer. He lost control of his vehicle, and it flipped over on its left side. Jeremy had his driver's side window open, and his left arm, hand and face all were injured as he and the vehicle slid along on the pavement.

There was a fatality in the accident. Jeremy's dog Major was in the back end of his pickup truck, and was thrown from the vehicle and killed when the vehicle flipped over.

I went to the scene, and there was a bunch of Jeremy's personal property strewn along the ramp. I grabbed a trash bag, and picked up as much of it as I could. Then, I took a recorded statement from the trucker who was still parked there. He told me that the young man had been taken by ambulance to the nearest hospital. So, I drove over the hospital to visit the young man and take him the bag of his belongings.

When I got there, I found a young man lying in a hospital bed with his head, left arm and left hand bandaged. He looked to be in pretty bad shape. I told him who I was, and asked him if he'd give me his statement. He agreed to do so.

Up to this point, this was a normal traffic accident.

The young man reached into the bag of belongings, and pulled out a notebook full of photographs. He showed me photos of Major, a Flying Disc-catching Border Collie. He also showed me a bunch of newspaper clippings about the dog. I learned that Major was a world champion disc-catching dog. I didn't even know that there was a world championship for dogs that caught flying discs, but there is. The photos and clippings showed all the places Major had performed and competed. This dog and the young man had even been featured a couple times at Superbowl football games.

But that was now only a memory, as Major was dead. Jeremy was heartbroken, because Major was his best friend. Together, Jeremy and Major had traveled all over the USA for flying disc competitions and performance appearances. They were members of the Greater Atlanta Dog and Disk Club, which I learned was the winningest Disc-Dog club on earth, with more champions than any other club in the world.

Who knew?

As Jeremy told me about the accident, I asked him what kind of money he was thinking about as a settlement. He told me that he wanted a new pickup, wanted his medical bills paid, wanted his lost income reimbursed. Then, he told me he wanted another $500 to buy another Border Collie puppy.

After Jeremy got out of the hospital, got back to work and things settled down, we totaled up his damages to his satisfaction. I reported this to the insurance company and recommended that they write this young man a check as soon as possible.

The last I heard, the insurance company wrote a settlement check quickly, and Jeremy got his new puppy.

CHAPTER NINETEEN

ADVANCE PAYMENTS

Often, when an insured has a loss of significant size, such as a residential hurricane loss or a fire, an advance payment of a portion of the anticipated settlement is issued by the insurance company. This situation also happens regularly when a business has a loss and needs money up front.

It is a customary and widely accepted practice for the insurance company to issue an advance payment in this type of instance. Be aware that there's nothing in the standard property insurance policy that deals with advances. It is usually just a courtesy that the insurance company extends to their policy owner.

However, they don't usually offer to do it. You have to request the advance.

Here's an example. Joe Smith's house is hit by lightning, and a fire damages most of the house. Joe's policy has Building limits of $100,000, Contents limits of $50,000, ALE limits of $20,000. The house can be repaired for $70,000, which is less than the policy limits. However, the adjuster expects that the Contents loss will exceed the policy limits of $50,000, and the ALE loss will be $15,000. The adjuster sends in his first report to the insurance company, and tells them to expect the loss to be approximately $135,000 on these three parts of coverage.

The insurance company could easily issue an initial advance payment of $25,000 to $35,000 for Contents and ALE, and $40,000 to $50,000 for the Dwelling loss.

So, what do you do if your Contents are damaged and you need the most basic things, like a change of clothes and shoes? What if you need to have a contractor secure the building and put tarps on the roof to keep further rain out of the building? Most people do not have tens of thousands of dollars just lying in their bank accounts that could be used to begin repairs, or begin replacing personal property. That's when the insurance company issues an advance.

It's best to make your request in writing. Even if it's just a hand-written letter, it's best if it's in writing. Write or type your request, keep a copy for your records, and give the copy to your adjuster. It's also a good idea to send a duplicate copy to the claims department of your insurance company. Send it by overnight courier or certified mail. NEVER rely on the adjuster to ask for an advance on your behalf. He might get delayed with other work and it could be days before he asks. DO IT YOURSELF.

Once the insurance company issues you the advance check, go to your bank and open a separate account just for handling claims issues.

Normally, when the insurance company issues advance payments against the ALE or Contents losses. the checks will be made payable just to you, because there's no mortgage on your contents.

When you ask for an advance against your Dwelling coverage, the insurance company will need to know the name and address of your mortgage company. They will issue the check jointly in your name and the name of the lender. They may send the check to you. If they do, the lender will likely require you to endorse the check and give the check to them. Then, they will set up a system of payments. To find out more about that system of payments, contact the Escrow Department of your Mortgage Company. Every lender is different. Find out what your lender plans to do.

DO NOT DEPOSIT THE ADVANCE CHECK IN YOUR NORMAL CHECKING OR SAVINGS ACCOUNT. Keeping a separate account for insurance claim related expenditures makes it so much easier to keep good records.

ONLY USE THIS MONEY FOR THE CLAIM. Don't take a weekend vacation to Las Vegas with the money, or buy yourself that new motorcycle you've always wanted.

When you receive the other payments for the claim, deposit them in this account. ONLY use this account for the expenses of the claim. When the claim is completed, close the account.

CHAPTER TWENTY

APPRAISAL CLAUSE

What if, after all you've done, you and your adjuster/insurance company are at an impasse on the value of your property? It's now time to invoke the Appraisal Clause in your insurance policy. The Appraisal Clause is usually found under the Heading "Conditions" and/or "What to do after a loss."

HERE'S A REALLY IMPORTANT TIP!!! You don't have to wait until you're hopelessly deadlocked with the adjuster or appraiser to invoke the Appraisal Clause. You can do it any time. I'm not suggesting that you become uncooperative. But occasionally, I talk to people who are having real difficulties with their adjuster or insurance company. Taking the claim to Appraisal sometimes stops all the drama.

Appraisal Clause is meant to be the method for determining disputed values. Appraisal cannot be used to determine what is covered. That is for a court of law to decide. If you have dispute with the company on whether or not something is covered, then you must file a lawsuit against your insurer to get that determination.

Here's what the Appraisal Clause reads in my Homeowner Insurance policy:

"If you and we fail to agree on the amount of loss, either may demand an appraisal of the loss. In this event, each party will choose a competent appraiser within 20 days after receiving a written request from the other. The two appraisers will choose an umpire. If they cannot agree upon an umpire within 15 days, you or we may request that the choice be made by a judge of a court of record in the state where the "residence premises" is located. The appraisers will separately set the amount of loss. If the appraisers submit an agreement to us, the amount agreed upon will be the amount of loss. If they fail to agree, they will submit their differences to the umpire. A decision agreed to by any two will set the amount of loss.

Each party will:
a. pay its own appraiser, and
b. Bear the other expenses of the appraisal and umpire equally."

Notice that there are very specific time limits in the Clause. You MAKE SURE that you choose your appraiser and notify the adjuster within the time limit in your policy. The time limit for both appraisers to choose an umpire begins on the day that both sides choose their appraiser.

Watch very carefully to see if the insurance company and/or adjuster chooses their appraiser within that time limit. If they do not, they have violated the terms and conditions of their policy.

The appraisers can still negotiate and reach an agreed amount of the damages. But, if they cannot agree, the case goes to the umpire. Then, if any two parties agree to the amount of the loss, that amount becomes the claim amount.

My recommendation, in the event of an appraisal, is to call an public adjusting company in your area. Ask for a licensed Public Adjuster. A PA is the best qualified person I can think of to be able to evaluate and appraise a dispute like this. The PA knows insurance policies, knows the Appraisal Clause, and knows property values. The PA is the perfect choice for helping you prove the values of the property of your claim.

CHAPTER TWENTY ONE

CO-INSURANCE

This chapter doesn't apply to automobile claims, but you should still read it!

There is one portion of a commercial or residential property insurance policy that is extra confusing to most policyholders. That is the issue of Co-insurance.

If you don't understand this part of the insurance contract, it can cost you thousands of dollars at claim time.

In a Homeowner policy, there is not usually a section entitled "Co-insurance." But the clause is listed in the Section I, Conditions, of the standard Homeowners HO-3 form.

Go find your policy and turn to the Conditions section, and read the part labeled "Loss Settlement." I thought about putting a copy of the section in this chapter to make it easy for you. But the reason I'm writing this book is to shake you up and get you more involved in your own claim. You're going to get paid hundreds or thousands of dollars more because of the stuff in this book, and you're not going to give me any of it. So, get busy and read your policy.

Let me at least translate the legalese: The insurance company requires you to carry policy limits on the Dwelling equal to no less than 80% of the full replacement cost of the building (not including foundations or underground pipes, wires or drains). If you do not carry 80% of the full replacement cost, the insurance company will penalize you when you have a claim.

Simple. But dangerous for your cash flow.

If you have a home that has a replacement cost of $100,000, and your policy limit for the Dwelling is $100,000...no penalty! You're insured 100% to value. You really should be insured 100% to value all the time.

Please remember that being insured to value does NOT mean that you insure your dwelling or building for its market value or sale price. Insure the dwelling or building for the amount of money it will take to rebuild the dwelling or building completely. Don't include the cost of the land your dwelling or building sits on. Insurance companies don't insure dirt.

In this example, you could be insured for as low as $80,000, and receive 100% of any claim with no penalty. However, you'd still be technically underinsured. In the case of a large loss, you would not collect all you should to make you whole again.

Insure your property for anything less than the percentage shown in your policy and there could be a coinsurance penalty.

There's a simple formula to figure co-insurance:

What you DID buy divided by what you SHOULD have bought.

$$\frac{DID}{SHOULD} \quad \text{x loss minus deductible = claim amount}$$

Here's a quick example:

The value of the property	$150,000
Coinsurance percentage	80%
The limit of insurance is	$100,000
The deductible amount is	$250
The amount of the loss is	$20,000

Step 1: $150,000 x 80% = $120,000 (the minimum amount of insurance to meet your coinsurance requirement)

Step 2: $100,000 (what you did) divided by $120,000 (should have done) = .67, or 67%

Step 3: $20,000 x 67% = $13,400

Step 4: $13,400 - $250 = $13,150

You see? It really is quite simple to figure out.

Sometimes, there is a coinsurance requirement on the Contents portion of the coverage, too. The same rule applies, and the same method of figuring out if there's a penalty applies.

The BIG problem is that most people don't figure out that there is a coinsurance problem until AFTER they have a loss of some kind.

There are a few obvious reasons that property is under-insured:

1. When you filled out your insurance application, you used a figure that is too low for replacement cost of your house. This could come from:

A. Ignorance…meaning you don't really know how much it would actually cost to replace your home.

B. Simply using the same policy limits on your new policy as you had on your old policy.

C. Being too cheap, and buying a policy with lower limits to save premium dollars.

2. Your agent doesn't know what it would cost to replace your house when he submits the application.

3. The agent was bidding low price to get your business, and made some cuts to get the premium down.

About the only thing that you can do to minimize a coinsurance penalty is to challenge it.

If your adjuster tells you that you will have a coinsurance penalty assessed against your claim, make him provide his calculations of the coinsurance penalty.

The first thing that the adjuster has to do to calculate coinsurance is to calculate the valuation of your property. EVERYTHING ELSE he does is based on that calculation. If it's too high, your coinsurance penalty will be too high.

He will calculate either the Replacement Cost Valuation (RCV) or he will calculate the Actual Cash Valuation (ACV). The policy will tell him which valuation to use. He doesn't get to choose on his own. Most Homeowners policies are RCV on the dwelling. Most commercial property is ACV, although an endorsement for RCV is available for a small extra premium.

To calculate the property valuation, the adjuster can use:

1. A Wild A** Guess (often done)
2. His estimating software. Some estimating software has valuation built in, so all he has to do is enter data about the age and condition, the size of the building, the features, etc., and that software will do the work for him.
3. Marshall and Swift (M&S). The absolute standard in the insurance industry for building valuation is a company called Marshall and Swift. All adjusters know about M&S, even if they don't know how to use their database. (If your adjuster doesn't know about M&S, or how to use it, get another adjuster FAST.) Even if the adjuster uses M&S, you need to review the data he entered to obtain the valuation. If he entered wrong data, the valuation will be wrong, too. For example, if he used the area of your house at 2,000 square feet, and your house is only 1,600 square feet, the entire valuation will be

wrong.

There are a bunch of variables that are entered into a valuation software program that have a DIRECT bearing on your valuation. Things like:

Age
Condition
Size
Number of rooms
Maintenance
Finishes and extras
Basement or slab foundation

SUPER HOT TIP!!!

YOU can now use the Marshall and Swift valuation program, just like an adjuster. They have built a website where any person can go and calculate their own property valuation. They charge about $8-$15 for each valuation. There is a tutorial on the home page of the website, which will tell you exactly how to use the program. It's super easy and very accurate.

Go to: http://www.swiftestimator.com

****

Remember, require your adjuster to furnish a copy of his valuation calculations for your property. Compare it with the Marshall and Swift valuation to make sure it's accurate. If you don't have the ability to get your own valuation, take the adjuster's valuation and show it to a real estate broker. Not just an agent, but a broker. The broker will likely be able to look at your property and the valuation, and tell you if it's accurate.

If you have calculated a lower valuation than the adjuster, insist that he use your valuation for his coinsurance calculations.

If you're reading this book BEFORE you have a claim, call your agent and make sure that you are insured to value.

If you're reading this book AFTER you have a claim, call your agent and ask him why you're NOT insured to value. If your agent messed up, and you can prove it, you could have grounds to make a claim against the Errors and Omissions Liability coverage of your agent.

If you're reading this book to figure out how to collect every dollar you're entitled to collect, then...

FIGHT FOR EVERY PERCENTAGE POINT!! Every percentage point of a coinsurance penalty is worth hundreds or thousands of dollars. Don't allow yourself to be cheated out of all of the money you are entitled to collect.

CHAPTER TWENTY TWO

MOLD CLAIMS

One of the big problems in mitigating a water loss is growth of mold and mildew. Getting the water damage repaired quickly can prevent mold and mildew. Mold and mildew can make a home uninhabitable, causing lots of different health problems, even death.

Take mold and mildew very seriously in your home. Just rubbing some chlorine bleach on it will only bleach out its color, just like when a brunette puts it on her hair.

Special mildewcides must be used to kill the spores and keep them from growing.

Sometimes, even that's not enough to get rid of mold. If the mold has become widespread, it could require major demolition and remodeling. Some molds, like *stachybotrys,* can cause death.

American insurance companies, almost in unison, have very quietly slipped in the Mold Exclusion endorsements into their policies since about 2003. Stunningly, the insurance buyers and consumer groups didn't notice this since the Terrorism Exclusion endorsements were introduced about the same time.

In 2001 and 2002, before mold claims were excluded, mold damage claims were filed with about the same number and severity as fire claims. It's almost as if the insurance companies excluded fire losses, because their exposure was about the same for mold and fire. If they had excluded fire, everyone from Congress on down would have been screaming for their heads on a pike.

Yet few people noticed when the mold exclusion happened.

These claims are basically Water Damage claims, and some type of water damage is still the cause of the loss. The mold grows on the organic material that gets wet, like drywall, wood sheathing and cellulose insulation.

Now, the old water damage claims for property damage can include Bodily Injury and legal defense costs.

There are hundreds of thousands of water damages claims every year. These claims are not going to just go away because the insurance company excluded coverage. The insurers have SHAMEFULLY shifted the cost of repairs to the policyowners and to their lenders.

By the way, if you have a mortgage on your property, it likely has a clause requiring you to provide "all-risk" or "extended peril" property coverage for your dwelling. If your policy now excludes Mold Damage, you are technically in default of your loan agreement. It would be best if you bought Mold Damage coverage BEFORE your lender finally notices the HUGE exposure in their loan portfolio, and requires you to buy the coverage.

Mold has already bankrupted more builders than any other type of casualty loss in history. And so far, Mold Damage Liability coverage for contractors and builders has not been easy to find.

Remember Ed McMahon? He is best known as the sidekick to

Johnny Carson of the Tonight Show on NBC. In 2002, McMahon sued his insurance company American Equity Insurance Co., for more than $20 million, asserting that toxic mold sickened him and his wife Pamela, killed their dog Muffy, and made their Beverly Hills house uninhabitable.

A pipe had broken in the six-bedroom home, flooding the family room. Mold spread throughout the house, even spreading into the heating and air conditioning ducts. The cleanup contractors just painted over some of the mold.

The suit was finally settled in 2003 for $7.2 million. This settlement is the highest published recovery in the United States by an individual filing for property damage in a mold lawsuit.

Lots of insurance companies have added a Mold and Microorganism Exclusion to their policies. Check your policy to see if mold is covered or excluded.

If it is excluded, start NOW finding coverage for Mold Damage.

If you had a water damage loss that ended up with mold, you should still be able to collect for the damage that the water did to your property BEFORE the mold grew. Don't just sit idly by and accept a mold claim denial from an insurance company. Go ahead and prove that the water damage happened FIRST, and get your claim paid. Even if you have to file a lawsuit, it could be worth it.

CHAPTER TWENTY THREE

RUSS HAS A WRECK!!

Can you imagine a better way to practice what I preach than with my own traffic accident? What better example could I give you than what I went through when I had a minor car wreck? Well, it actually happened during the time I was writing this book.

<u>WATCH CAREFULLY</u> for the strategies in this chapter. They will be reiterated again later in case you miss then.

About 4:30 on a sunny Thursday afternoon in October, I was driving from my office to my home. I was on a city street that had two lanes going one way, a median in the middle (where else would they put the median?) and two lanes going the other way. I was in the far right lane. Rush hour traffic was moving along about 30 miles per hour, and we were about 100 yards from a traffic light.

Suddenly, the white Ford Explorer directly in front of me jammed on his brakes and slowed rapidly. I hit my brakes, and was confident that I was not going to hit him in the rear.

I glanced in my rear view mirror, and instantly realized that the

Lexus behind me wasn't going to stop in time.

I braced for impact.

He finally noticed that traffic was stopped ahead of him, but it was too late for him to stop safely. In the mirror I watched him slam on his brakes, and saw the front end of his car dive downward…just before it hit my rear bumper. The impact pushed my Cadillac Deville forward about three feet, into the trailer hitch on the Ford Explorer.

It was all over in perhaps three seconds…but, in reality, it had only just begun.

I turned on my emergency flashers, and shifted into "Park." I grabbed my cell phone and dialed 911. The operator answered and I reported the accident. I opened the glovebox, and retrieved my registration and insurance certificate. I reached for the camera that I usually keep in the glovebox, but it wasn't there. (I had taken it out a few days before, and forgotten to put it back) Meanwhile, the driver of the Explorer had gotten out of his vehicle and had looked at his rear bumper and trailer hitch.

I got out of my car and walked to the front. The impact had been severe enough to knock the lenses off of the headlights, and the lenses were lying on the pavement. Curiously, though, the impact was not enough to deploy the airbag. There was a nice square hole in the front of my plastic bumper where it struck the Explorer's trailer hitch receiver. I walked over to the sidewalk, about eight feet from my car.

The Explorer driver joined me on the sidewalk. I asked him if he was injured, and he said he was not. I handed him two of my business cards, and asked him to write his name and address on the back of one of the cards, and keep one. He said that he could not find any damage to his vehicle, and did not want to stay around.

The Lexus driver came to the sidewalk where we were standing. I handed him two of my business cards, and asked for his name, address and phone number. He looked at my business card, and said,

"You're an insurance adjuster?"

"Yes," I answered, "and it looks like you're just about to have a real bad day."

The Explorer driver said goodbye, and started to leave. I urged him not to leave the scene of the accident, but he left anyway. I'll always wonder why he was so eager to go.

About then, a police cruiser arrived, and the officer asked us to move our vehicles to the parking lot on the other side of the sidewalk. He collected our documents, asked us about the accident details, and then went to his cruiser to write the ticket for the Lexus driver.

In about fifteen minutes, the officer got out of his cruiser, handed me my documents, handed the Lexus driver his documents and a nice ticket for failure to maintain safe distance, and then the officer left the scene.

Both of our cars could still be driven safely, so I wished the other driver "good luck" and drove home.

Once I got home, I took my digital camera outside and photographed the Caddy from all four corners, all four side views, and close-up views of the damage. Then, I came in to my home office and picked up a cassette recorder and a new tape. I then dictated a statement with as much detail as I could think of regarding the accident.

Then I reached into my credenza and picked up a manila file folder. I stapled an empty envelope inside, into which I placed the police officer's card with the accident report number, and the business card that had the other driver's contact information. Then, I attached three pages of a legal pad that I could use as a diary. (Thoughout the claim process, I wrote down every phone call, time, date, and what was said. I also wrote down every conversation in person, and what was said.)

I stapled another envelope inside the folder, and into it I placed the cassette tape and camera memory disc and sealed it.

By bedtime that evening, my neck was getting pretty sore, and I found that I'd been injured, even though I felt no injury at the accident site.

The next day, I called the other driver's insurance company and reported a claim. The other driver had not reported the claim yet. I was told that a claims representative would contact me within a couple days.

I also called my own insurance company and reported the claim, even though the other driver was at fault. (Remember in Chapter Five you learned that you must report your accident to your own insurance company. Failure to do so could jeopardize your right to be defended by your own insurer.)

I called my attorney, and informed him that I had been in a traffic accident. I gave him the details, and told him that I would be calling him regularly as the claims process continued. Because my injuries were very minor, we agreed that there was no need for me to retain him to complete the claim, but that he would oversee the claims process to assure that I did not sign anything that relinquished any of my rights.

At lunchtime, I drove to my chiropractor's office. He did a full series of X-rays on my neck and upper back, and did a chiropractic treatment. He stated that he thought I had sustained a mild soft-tissue injury that would respond well to treatment. He recommended that I begin therapy with two treatments per week for the first two weeks, with re-evaluations as healing progressed.

After work, I drove my car to the local Cadillac dealer body shop. I asked the service writer to inspect the car and write an estimate, making sure that his estimate included Original Equipment Manufacturer (OEM) parts. He said that he was very familiar with the other insurance company and that the other insurance company would <u>never</u> agree to OEM parts. But he did write the estimate the way I asked. The estimate he wrote totaled $3,474.13.

On Saturday, I went back to the accident scene at about 4:30. (Why the same time as the accident? So that the daylight would be the same as the day of the accident for the photos I would take). I drew a diagram of the roadway, with all lanes, turn lanes, median, traffic signs, businesses and adjoining streets shown on the drawing. I did not measure with a tape, but simply stepped off the distances as my unit of measurement. I took my camera with me, and photographed the scene from four different angles.

I received my first call from the other insurance company on the next Tuesday. The examiner left a message on my voicemail. (Throughout the claims process, I did not ever accept a phone call directly from the examiner, the auto appraiser, or the body shop. I let the call go to my voicemail. Once I had hooked up the cassette recorder so that I could record the conversation, I returned the call.) The examiner identified herself, and verified the accident information. She asked me if she could take a recorded statement, and I told her that I would agree to a recorded statement if it were taken in the office of my attorney. She agreed, and I gave her the name and phone number of my attorney.

The examiner said that the auto appraiser for their company would contact me in a day or so, and that he would make an appointment to inspect the vehicle. Two days later, the appraiser called, and I met him in the parking lot at my office. I took my mini-cassette recorder with me, and began recording when we met. I turned the recorder off after the appraiser was done, and we had parted company. The tape went into the file folder. I also gave him a copy of the body shop estimate.

At this point, he mentioned that the body shop estimate listed OEM parts. I replied that the vehicle was manufactured to strict government standards, and those standards were only met with OEM parts. He said his company would pay for aftermarket parts, not OEM. I asked him if his company would pay to have the vehicle recertified as safe once the aftermarket parts were installed. He said "no."

"In that case," I answered, "isn't it in the best interests of your company and my safety to repair the vehicle with OEM parts? The only way that my vehicle can be returned to pre-loss condition is if OEM parts are used."

He agreed, and wrote his estimate. It actually turned out to be a few dollars more than the body shop estimate, and specified OEM parts.

IMPORTANT NOTE!!   Many times, the insurance company will try to insist on aftermarket parts. Don't allow them to bully you!! They'll tell you that if you want to have OEM parts installed on your damaged vehicle, you'll have to pay the difference. What I've just showed you is the principle found in Chapter Twenty Four that the insurance company CANNOT return your vehicle to pre-loss condition without using OEM parts. The examiner may want to depreciate the parts, and this is also negotiable.

The next day, the examiner called me and authorized the body shop to repair my car. She also authorized a rental car during the time my car would be in the body shop. The car she authorized, although not a full-sized car, was a mid-size Chevy Malibu that was acceptable.

By this day, I'd picked up a copy of the police report, and sent a copy by fax to the examiner.

On Friday afternoon…one week later…I dropped my car at the body shop, and picked up my rental car.

The next Friday, the body shop called and said my vehicle was ready. After work, I dropped by the dealership, and pulled my car out into the parking lot. I took the body shop estimate, and inspected each item, checking off each item on the estimate that had been repaired. I found that one of the headlight assemblies that was supposed to be replaced had only been cleaned up and glued together. I showed the shop manager, and he apologized for the error.

He said I could drive the vehicle home, and simply bring it back on Monday to have the assembly replaced. I turned in my rental car and drove my Caddy to the house.

On Monday, I took the car back to the dealership, and they drove me to my office. They replaced the headlight assembly, and at lunchtime, they sent a car over to get me. I did the inspection over again, and endorsed the settlement check and paid the repair bill in full.

Notice here that <u>I did not pay the repair bill until I was satisfied that the repairs were completed to my satisfaction</u>. This was an unusual situation where the body shop manager allowed me to take the vehicle home for the weekend. Normally, the body shop won't let you do that. However, you should test drive the vehicle before you sign off on it. I don't mean once around the parking lot, either. I mean a comprehensive test drive to see if it works the way it did before the accident. Acceleration, braking, handling, fit and finish, paint appearance, A/C and/or heater operation, how the engine sounds and runs...all of these things and more should be evaluated BEFORE you accept the vehicle and pay the bill. A driving test like that should take you at least thirty minutes.

If you don't feel qualified to make this evaluation, get a mechanic from another dealership or body shop to ride with you while you evaluate the car's condition. It may cost you a few dollars, but it will be money well spent.

Three weeks have gone by at this point, and my neck was healing up pretty well. By the fourth week, I only had one chiropractic treatment, and the doctor released me from treatment. He stated that he had done as much as possible, and was satisfied with the progress back to wellness.

His secretary gave me the final bill in the amount of $880.00.

I spoke to my attorney again, and he stated that, in this instance...because I am an adjuster, he did not think it necessary to give a recorded statement with his supervision. So, I called the examiner and recorded the phone interview myself at the same time she was recording the interview. I put the tape in the file folder.

It was time for me to calculate my claim, and determine the range of compensation in which I'd settle the claim with the insurance company. We'd already settled on the Property Damage portion of the claim, so the only portion left was the Bodily Injury portion.

Medical bills are referred to as "Special Damages", or just "Specials". For decades, the insurance claims adjusters and examiners have used a commonly accepted multiplier of 3 for figuring out an uncomplicated settlement.

For example, if a claimant has medical bills of $1,000.00, it is not unusual for the insurance company to make their first offer two times specials ($2,000.00). This is customary on small, uncomplicated claims. If the claimant accepts it, the insurance company saved a bunch of money, and can close the claim quickly. However, if the claimant objects, the insurance company is still very comfortable with a settlement of three times specials, or $3,000.00.

When the claim becomes complicated, the use of that multiplier goes away, and the attorneys take over.

In my case, my specials totaled $880.00. Multiplied times three, the total is $2,640.00. Multiplied times four, the total is $3,520.00. I made the decision that I would start negotiations with an offer to settle of $3,520.00, and accept no less than $2,640.00.

The claims examiner agreed to settle at $2,640.00. I picked up the check, exchanging it for a signed release form, and the claim was finally settled for a grand total of $6,114.00.

This is a small claim, and was easily settled. But the reason it was easily settled is that I was prepared to handle the claims process myself, and did not allow the insurance company to establish the rules.

If I had not been in control, the insurance company could have installed aftermarket parts on the car, saving themselves about $500.00. The examiner made her first offer to settle specials for $1,500.00. If I had accepted that amount, they would have saved another $1,140.00.

Add those two together, and the total is $1,640.00. That is over 26% of the total amount of the claim.

That is the amount of money that I was entitled to collect…that I would not have collected if I wasn't prepared.

The one thing that I regret in the process is that I was not completely prepared. I didn't have a camera in the glovebox of the Caddy on the day of the accident. Those on-scene photos could have been crucial if there were any dispute about the details of the accident. I just got lucky that the photos were not needed.

Since then, I bought a cellular phone that has a built-in camera. Now, I have a camera with me everywhere I go.

As you have just read, even a seasoned claims adjuster can get caught unprepared for a traffic accident. But with the information you've found in this book about how to handle yourself and your auto accident, you can be prepared, and know what to do WHEN it happens to you.

CHAPTER TWENTY FOUR

COLLISION CLAIMS

I'm telling you these steps to protect YOU. Failure to do these steps could cost you hundreds of thousands of dollars in a judgment or settlement that goes against you.

I've written many words and phrases in capital letters for emphasis, so you'll understand how crucial this information is.

Here are the steps to take when you're in a traffic accident:

ON SCENE - <u>BEFORE YOU GET OUT OF YOUR CAR OR TALK TO ANYONE!</u>

1. <u>**NEVER**</u> SAY IT WAS YOUR FAULT, **NEVER** ACCEPT BLAME OR ACCEPT LIABILITY…<u>NOT EVER…NEVER</u>.

2. AN APOLOGY IS AN ACCEPTANCE OF LIABILITY. UNDER NO CIRCUMSTANCES SHOULD YOU APOLOGIZE TO THE OTHER DRIVER, HIS PASSENGERS OR EVEN PASSENGERS IN YOUR OWN CAR. DON'T APOLOGIZE TO THE POLICE OFFICER, THE WRECKER DRIVER, THE

AMBULANCE TECHNICIAN…NOBODY. Acknowledge that it happened…if you must say something, say you regret <u>that it happened</u>, cry if you must…but DON'T APOLOGIZE.

3. Make sure everyone in YOUR CAR is OK. Find out if you or your passengers are injured. Once you take care of those in YOUR CAR, then you could see about the other car(s).

4. If you can, call the police and report your accident and injuries.

5. Get your driver's license, car registration and proof of insurance out, ready to present them to the police officer.

6. If it's possible, get yourself and your passengers to a safe place, such as the side of the road, out of the traffic lanes. If it is too dangerous to cross active lanes of traffic to get to safety, STAY INSIDE THE CAR.

7. When the officer arrives on the scene, be cooperative, but don't volunteer information. If the officer asks you if you are at fault, I recommend that you tell him you do not know. That is an entirely true statement. You are not the person or court of law that would determine who is at fault. Neither is the police officer, even if somebody gets a ticket. You may think you're at fault, but may not be legally at fault. Even if you get a ticket that does not necessarily prove that you are at fault. The law in some states has statutes of comparative negligence, which means you might only be found partially at fault, or not at all.

8. If you have a camera, or a cell phone with a camera, take as many photos as you can of:

a. The vehicles. If it's a multiple vehicle accident, you'll have a photo record of the description of each auto. Take shots of each license plate. Try to get photos before the cars are moved from the point of impact, if you can. If one vehicle is a commercial   vehicle, like an 18-wheeler, take a photo of the writing on the driver's door.

b. The damages. I've seen claimants try to get paid for damages having nothing to do with the accident.

c. The accident scene. Crucial evidence at an accident scene can be destroyed quickly. Skid marks can wear off, or can wash off with the first rain.

d. The wrecker. I've seen wreckers send a bill to the insurance company for accidents they didn't work.

e. The other driver and passengers. That way, you'll know who was involved, how many were involved, what they look like, and maybe their injuries will show. I've seen claims where people swore they were passengers in one of the cars, and were not even there.

9. Don't argue with the police officer. If you get a ticket, just sign it and accept it. Your attorney can deal with it later, but at the roadside, you'll probably not be successful.

10. DON'T SIGN ANYTHING ELSE AT THE ACCIDENT SCENE...NO MATTER WHO INSISTS ON GETTING YOUR SIGNATURE.

11. DON'T GIVE A RECORDED STATEMENT TO ANYONE AT THE ACCIDENT SCENE, NO MATTER WHO ASKS FOR IT. Tell them you'll give your statement in the presence of your attorney.

12. DON'T GIVE A WRITTEN STATEMENT AT THE ACCIDENT SCENE...NO MATTER WHO ASKS FOR IT. Tell them you'll give your statement in the presence of your attorney.

LATER, AFTER THE ACCIDENT.

1. Call your insurance company and notify them of your involvement in the accident. Make sure you notify them the way they require in the policy. Even if you are not at fault, you MUST notify YOUR insurance company. If you do not, you could be in violation

of the terms of your insurance policy, and become ineligible for the insurance company to defend you.

2. Call your Attorney. Tell the attorney the details of the accident. He can then advise you of the procedure you should undertake, and advise you of your legal rights. See Chapter Six, "Should I Get a Lawyer?"

3. Read Chapter Twenty Three, "Russ Has a Wreck." In that chapter, I tell you the procedure I used in the small auto accident I was in. Do what I did.

4. Read Chapters Twenty Five, Twenty Six and Twenty Seven.

DO WHAT IT SAYS TO DO!!

CHAPTER TWENTY FIVE

RECORDED STATEMENTS

I've taken hundreds of recorded statements over the years, and I know all of the tricks. People are so trusting, and will usually cooperate with the requests of someone they consider to be "official." Adjusters and claims examiners usually get that kind of deference from people, and I've never understood why. It probably has to do with the reason I wrote this book, which is that most people don't know much about their insurance policy and the claims process. They defer to the ones who know about it, and the ones who control the checkbooks.

Recorded statements are a normal part of the claims process. Claims adjusters usually like to get a recorded statement from all the parties in the loss early in the claims process. That way, the details of the claim are still fresh in everyone's minds, and can be documented more accurately. Don't be nervous about being recorded.

If the claims adjuster calls and requests a recorded statement over the telephone, politely tell him that you prefer to meet with him in person. The best scenario for you would be to meet the adjuster at your attorney's office, and give the recorded statement in the presence of the attorney. Even uncooperative or moody adjusters seem to be on their best behavior in the presence of an attorney.

If the insurance adjuster or examiner only does recorded statements by phone, simply have the adjuster do a three-way conference call with you and your attorney.

On an in-person interview, the adjuster will have his portable tape recorder with which he will record the interview. You should also bring a portable tape recorder and tape the interview for your own protection. You can buy a hand-sized cassette recorder at any electronics store or discount department store...even major drug store chains for less than $40.00. They use standard cassette tapes and batteries. The microcassette recorders work great, too, and cost about the same. Make sure that you have plenty of fresh batteries and a few cassette tapes with you at the interview.

When the adjuster is recording your statement, don't OFFER any information. Answer the question that he asked, and no more.

Remember that some questions do not deserve an answer.

Have you ever been in an interview, or some social situation, and someone asked you a question that made you uncomfortable? And you ANSWERED the question so they didn't think you were impolite? Then later you hated yourself for being a doormat?

People feel a need to be nice. Adjusters take advantage of people's need to be nice. Adjusters know that most people will answer whatever questions seem reasonable, even if the question is not relevant to the claim. Personal questions that do not have relevance to your claim should not be answered. Questions about your income, or asking for your Social Security number, may not be relevant to the claim. Questions about your income, for example, are not appropriate unless you are making a claim for lost wages.

One of the reasons that adjusters ask for your Social Security number is so they can look you up on a database called Insurance

Service Office (ISO) Claimsearch. If you want to see what the Claimsearch homepage looks like, go to: https://claimsearch.iso.com/index.asp

Claimsearch is a searchable database that shows if you've ever had an insurance claim before. With your Social Security number, adjusters and claims examiners can call up all the data about you...WITHOUT YOUR PERMISSION.

If there's a question that the adjuster asks that you don't feel comfortable answering, politely reply "I'd rather not answer that question." Sometimes adjusters ask inappropriate questions. Make sure that the adjuster sticks to the details of the accident or loss. If you're in an attorney's office at the time of the recorded statement, he'll help the adjuster stay on track.

My belief is that you, the policyholder or claimant, should record every telephone conversation and face-to-face conversation that you have with anyone about your claim. The same electronics stores that sell the cassette recorders will stock a "pick-up" microphone that plugs into your cassette recorder and has a suction cup that sticks to your telephone handset. The quality of the sound is usually quite good.

I'm not suggesting for a moment that you should do something illegal or unethical. You need to check your state's statutes and laws about recording conversations. Some states do not allow it unless both parties give consent. Some states allow it if only one of the parties is aware that the conversation is being recorded.

Know the law, and know your rights.

Don't be surprised if some people refuse to have their conversations recorded. That doesn't mean that you should cave in to their lack of cooperation. You should insist on the recording, or politely refuse to speak with that person. But, it should tell you something about that person if he or she refuses to be recorded.

Be in control of when and where you accept phone calls about your claim. I've seen some adjusters that try to keep the insured off balance by making calls at unusual times, like early morning or late night. If you're not ready to record the call when the phone rings, tell the person that it's not convenient to speak right then and make an appointment to call him back. <u>Always keep your appointments</u>.

I can imagine that some of you reading this chapter think that this author is some sort of paranoid kook. <u>Please let me assure you that I am</u>. But I've seen countless situations in which an adjuster took a recorded statement, and then wrote a statement summary that wasn't anything like the information on the tape. I've seen police officers fill out an accident report, and describe the accident completely wrongly. I've seen court testimony where the adjuster and the insured are questioned about an incident, and their stories are completely different.

Recordings of conversations put all of that to rest.

After you have a problem with a person who lies to you, or about you, it's too late to record them then.

The old adage is, "better safe than sorry." Sorry can cost you thousands of dollars.

CHAPTER TWENTY SIX

COMPREHENSIVE CLAIMS

"Comprehensive" is what this coverage used to be called. Sometimes, you'll find that your insurance policy calls this coverage "Other Than Collision." In this chapter, we'll refer to it as OTC.

Here are the events that are covered perils in a standard ISO auto policy under Section D, "Coverage for Damage to Your Auto:"

- Missiles or falling objects
- Hail, water or flood
- Fire
- Malicious mischief or vandalism
- Theft or larceny
- Riot or civil commotion
- Explosion or earthquake
- Contact with a bird or animal
- Windstorm
- Breakage of glass

If the glass breakage is caused by a collision, you can elect to have it paid under the Collision coverage. This will save you having to pay your OTC deductible as well as a Collision deductible. <u>That is a good thing!</u>

So, if you have a collision loss and glass gets broken, watch carefully that your insurance company or adjuster doesn't try to assess more than one deductible!

Mike, a good friend of mine, was driving his car along a rural road in deep South Georgia one sultry summer day. He was traveling about 65 mph, and came over the crest of a gentle hill. Just over the crest of that hill was a squashed possum ("opossum" for y'all that don't live in the South). Making a mid-day meal out of this possum were three turkey buzzards. When they saw Mike's car crest that hill, they did what comes naturally to turkey buzzards...they started to fly. Mike had no time to react. Unfortunately they were just about windshield height when Mike hit them, destroying his windshield and scaring the life out of him. The buzzards had a bad day, too.

The insurance company paid to replace the windshield from the OTC coverage. But, Mike is still a little twitchy when he sees birds while he's driving.

EXCLUSIONS

There are a whole bunch of exclusions under the OTC coverage. READ <u>YOUR </u>POLICY to see what's excluded from <u>your</u> coverage. One of the biggest problems people have with OTC coverage is when something gets stolen out of their vehicle.

OTC excludes most electronics, such as radios, tape players, CD players and now I-Pods. Computers, like laptops, are also excluded. Likewise CB radios, scanners and radar detectors. A latecomer to the OTC exclusion dance is the DVD players that parents use to keep the kids quiet when they're in the car. All of your tapes, CDs and DVDs are also not covered.

So, you could be driving around with hundreds, even thousands of dollars worth of electronics entertainment equipment in your ride.

HERE'S THE BIG CATCH!!!

The exclusion is for PORTABLE electronic equipment. The electronics PERMANENTLY INSTALLED in your car, even aftermarket installations, ARE USUALLY COVERED.

HOWEVER...

What do you do if your jewel-encrusted iPod gets stolen out of your vehicle?

Sorry, no coverage under your OTC coverage, BUT...

Look to your Homeowner's policy, or your Renter's policy!! Those policies usually cover your personal property <u>anywhere in the world</u>. You might have a larger deductible in your Homeowners policy than you had in your Auto policy, but some coverage is better than NO COVERAGE.

Wouldn't you agree?

SPEAKING OF COVERAGE...

The OTC Coverage in your Auto policy pays ACTUAL CASH VALUE for damaged or stolen property. That means that the adjuster will deduct money from the replacement cost for the age and condition of your damaged or stolen property. So, if your high-end Blauplunkt eight-speaker sound system gets stolen out of your car, you'll only get the DEPRECIATED VALUE for the system.

BE SURE to read Chapter Fifteen on how to handle Depreciation. This is a coverage where you can get RIPPED OFF EASILY!!

If your Homeowners policy has a Replacement Cost Endorsement on Personal Property coverage, you've proven how smart a consumer you are!! That means that the insurance company will replace your damaged or stolen property with property of like kind and quality, or they'll pay you money to buy property of like kind and quality. As I mentioned above, your deductible might be higher, but RCV is higher than ACV, so you'll likely collect more money.

Let's make up a story to give an example. Burt and Margaret and their three kids, ages 10, 12, and 15, are on a two week vacation in their SUV. Inside the car are four iPods, two laptops, 50 CDs, 20 DVDs, a portable boom box, three DVD players and two transistor radios.

They arrive at their destination in Florida and check in at the hotel. In the morning, they come out to get into their car, and find that a rear window has been broken out, and all of their electronics are gone. All of them.

Burt calls his insurance company and reports the theft. They tell him he has no coverage for portable electronics.

Burt is very unhappy. He already misses the quiet that he experienced on the ride down to Florida, and knows it will not be like that going home.

However, after the vacation is over, Burt gets home and goes to his bedside table, where a copy of this book is kept next to his Bible. He is reminded that his Homeowners policy does cover the stolen property. He smiles broadly, calls his Homeowner agent and files a claim. His homeowner policy has a $500 deductible.

The list is like this:

QTY.	ITEM	EACH	AGE	RCV	DEPR	ACV
4	iPods	$180	2 yr	$ 720	$240	$480
2	laptops	$699	3 yr	$1398	$699	$699
50	CDs	$ 12	2 yr	$ 600	$300	$300
20	DVD	$ 20	1 yr	$ 400	$160	$240
1	boombox	$159	3 yr	$ 159	$ 80	$ 79
3	DVD players	$139	1 yr	$ 417	$120	$297

2	radios	$ 39	2 yr	$ 78	$ 39	$ 39
	TOTALS			$3,772	$1,638	$2,134
	Less deductible					($500)
	ACV claim amount					$1,634
	Recoverable depreciation					$1,638

The insurance company will pay the ACV of $1,634 up front. Then, when he has replaced all of the electronics and shows the insurance company the receipts, they will send him a check for the remaining $1,638.00.

In this example, I just did "WAG" estimates on depreciation, just like your adjuster will likely do. Electronics have a pretty short useful life, and depreciate quickly. The method that your adjuster uses to determine depreciation should be able to be documented. Make him prove it.

Still, in this example, Burt and Margaret got paid $3,272 for their stolen electronics through their Homeowner policy that was not covered under the Auto policy.

BEWARE!

ALL of the non-electronics personal property that is in your car, like your clothing, or jewelry, or cameras...will be adjusted on an ACV basis. So, if your non-electronics personal property is insured through your Homeowners policy, you might consider making your claim through that policy instead of your Auto policy.

This coverage also extends to any "non-owned auto." That could mean a rental car., or a loaner car.

THE OTHER MAJOR PROBLEM AREA WITH OTC COVERAGE IS...

Theft of your vehicle.

The insurance company and adjuster are going to try their best to pay you the lowest ACV price for your car. They'll use the Kelly Blue Book, or the Black Book or some method of determining the value of your car. But, there are a lot of variables to the value of a vehicle, like:

- you're meticulous, and detail your car regularly. You only use the dealership for service, and you've kept all the receipts for services since you bought the car. Your vehicle is worth more than an average vehicle.

- you had aftermarket customizing done to your car...like air dams and spoilers, or custom seats and seat covers.

- you had a custom paint job on your vehicle.

- you only drove your car in good weather, kept it garaged, and it had never been rained on.

With just these variables, you can see that the average price for your make and model that goes through the local auto auction is not going to be acceptable to you. There could easily be hundreds of dollars of difference between what you KNOW your vehicle is worth, and what the insurance company and adjuster think it's worth.

IN CASES LIKE THIS...rely on your documentation and photos of your vehicle. You do have photos of your car, don't you?

Or, what if you have an ordinary car with average miles on it, and you still don't think that the adjuster is being fair with you on the amount of settlement?

Carefully document the make, model, mileage and condition of your car. Go online and get a photo of what your car looked like. Or, go to a dealership and find a car that is as closely alike to your car as possible, and take a photo. Add in your Bill of Sale for your vehicle which shows what you paid for it.

Then take this file of information to three to five automobile dealers (I like five better), and ask to speak to the Used Car Manager. Make sure at least two of those dealers sell the make of your car. For example, if your car was an Audi, go see Audi dealers. Tell him you need a written appraisal of the vehicle based upon the information in the file.

Once you get that information you'll have a range of prices from lowest to highest. Start negotiating with the adjuster from the highest price. If he accepts your high price, fine. If he makes counter offers, come down on your offer in increments of $50.00 until you and he reach agreement.

Just remember, once you've made an offer, SHUT UP until the adjuster either accepts or makes a counter offer.

If nothing works, and you cannot come to agreement, send the insurance company a written certified letter invoking the Appraisal Clause in the policy. Each party chooses a competent appraiser, and the appraisers agree on an umpire. An agreement between any two will be binding, and you'll have your fairest price for your vehicle.

SURE, IT'S A LOT OF WORK...but don't you want to be SURE you are in charge, and don't you want the peace of mind to KNOW that NOBODY RIPPED YOU OFF?

You can do this, my friend!!

CHAPTER TWENTY SEVEN

DIMINISHED VALUE

Insurance companies really hate this topic. Let's explore it, and then you'll know how it could affect you if you have any kind of a collision loss.

In this chapter, I'm going to refer to all cars, trucks, motorcycles, boats, RVs, anything you can drive, as "vehicles."

Vehicles of every type depreciate. For those of you not familiar with that term, it simply means that vehicles lose their value over time. Most everyone has had the experience of buying a car for a certain price, and then finding out five years later that, when you try to sell the car, it's worth far less than when you bought it.

Chapter Fifteen deals with depreciation. Don't forget to read it.

Remember that depreciation is affected by time, but also by the condition of the vehicle. If you keep your vehicle in perfect condition, it will depreciate more slowly than a vehicle that's not in such pristine condition. But it's still going to depreciate.

Even if your vehicle is maintained perfectly, the value of your vehicle will shrink if it has been in an accident.

Diminished value (DV) is the loss in market value that happens when a vehicle is damaged and then repaired. Think about this example: if you were looking at two identical vehicles with the idea of buying one of them...and one had been wrecked and repaired, even extremely well repaired, and the other vehicle had no damage...and they were the same price...which one would you want to buy? You'd probably choose the one with no damage.

Next question: how much of a discount off the selling price would you have to get to give serious consideration to buying the car that had the damage? Well, that discount is, in essence, the "diminished value" of that repaired vehicle.

The principle in the law of Diminished Value has a long and generally accepted history. That hasn't stopped the insurance industry, however. The insurance companies have been denying DV claims for years, and they'll continue to deny claims for DV. Some insurance companies LIE about the law. Let me show you how.

In the State of Georgia, there was a landmark court case about DV called Mabry v. State Farm. On November 28, 2001 the case was handed down from the Georgia Supreme Court. The decision stated that ALL insurance companies doing business in the State of Georgia had to pay diminished value as a part of the collision claim. The parties IN THIS CASE agreed to use a formula to calculate the diminished value, called the "17C formula."

The "17C formula" was ONLY MEANT for the two parties in that particular case. There is nothing in the ruling that directs EVERYBODY to use the "17C formula." The formula was crafted by the insurance companies to lower the amount they would have to pay in any DV loss.

These days, many insurance companies flatly refuse to pay DV. If they do give it consideration, they will try to use the "17C formula" in the calculation of the claim. They might even try to refer to the Georgia Supreme Court case as their precedent.

If your vehicle is damaged in an accident, the insurance company owes you money for Diminished Value. <u>There is no state in the USA where this is NOT TRUE.</u>

The foremost experts in the nation about Diminished Value are here in the Atlanta area. Their business is called Collision Claim Associates, Inc., in Cumming, Georgia. They serve clients in all 50 states. Their website is crammed full of extremely important information about Diminished Value, and how you can collect every dollar that you're entitled to collect. They offer a FREE DV claim review at the site. If you want a full written report, they charge a fee for that.

I strongly recommend these guys!! Go to my website and click on the link to their website.

There is another very serious issue that I wrote briefly about in Chapter Twenty Three, "Russ Has a Wreck." That is the safety of your repaired vehicle. <u>This safety issue directly affects Diminished Value.</u>

In the automotive parts industry, there is something called "Aftermarket Parts." Depending on whom you ask, these parts are equal, better or worse than the Original Equipment Manufacturer parts. These are parts not necessarily manufactured to Original Equipment Manufacturer (OEM) specifications. They are NOT OEM parts. In most cases, they are inferior parts, and cost much less than OEM parts. One of the reasons they are cheaper is that they are not subject to the same crash testing procedures as OEM and therefore are not as safe.

The auto manufacturers get safety certification from the US Federal Government for their products. That means that every part that goes into a vehicle has to pass strict government standards.

Aftermarket parts may be interchangeable in repairs, but they are NOT OEM parts.

That means that, if you repair your vehicle with aftermarket parts, it would not pass a Federal inspection for safety.

If you plan on reselling or trading your car, you should seriously consider only using OEM parts. These days, anyone with an internet connection and the vehicle identification number can check your vehicle's damage repair history. All they have to do is go to www.carfax.com . Body shops and insurance companies report damages to Carfax, and it goes into their database.

The trade-in value of your car, repaired with aftermarket parts, could be significantly diminished. Also, using non-OEM parts to repair a leased car could cost you all or part of your security deposit, since you won't be returning the vehicle to the dealer in the same condition as when you took delivery of the vehicle.

Insurance companies don't really care about your safety. For the most part, the insurance companies will encourage you to use aftermarket parts to repair your vehicle after a wreck. In fact, some insurance companies state that they will only pay for aftermarket parts.

A few insurance companies, such as Chubb Insurance, actually encourage their policyholders to use OEM parts, while not charging them a penalty.

Insurance claims are designed to return your property to its pre-loss condition, if possible. If your vehicle was an OEM vehicle prior to the accident, then the ONLY WAY to return your vehicle to its pre-loss condition is to use OEM parts.

Anything else is allowing the insurance company to rip you off!!

If your vehicle had been damaged before, and you're now replacing aftermarket parts with more aftermarket parts, there's not a lot that can be argued about the safety issue. I'd still recommend that you replace the damaged aftermarket parts with OEM in order to return your car to its safest condition. It might cost you some money over and above the insurance payment, but you'd be safer.

So, in ANY accident…whether you're at fault, or some one else is at fault, INSIST on OEM parts for the repair of your vehicle. Fight for it! Call the State Department of Insurance and file a complaint. Call the local Consumer radio or TV talk show and tell your story. Call the local newspaper and try to get them to do a story about your experience.

Fight and WIN!!

CHAPTER TWENTY EIGHT

DUCK!!

I got a liability claim assignment a few years ago regarding a woman who had been injured at a concert here at a large outdoor venue in Atlanta. That sounds somewhat normal, doesn't it? Well, this claim was anything but normal.

The insured was a very well known American rock band. If I gave you their name, you'd certainly recognize it. The claimant was a young wife and mother, about 37 years old at that time. She was married to a handsome young man who was both an attorney and a magistrate judge. She was beautiful…about 5'-4", honey colored long hair, slender and willowy. Let's call her Susan (not her real name). We'll call her husband Don (not his real name either).

Don knew that Susan really liked the music of this particular band. So, Don bought two tickets in the second row from the edge of the stage.

On the night of the concert, they excitedly took their places at their seats. However, they stood for most of the concert, just like the others around them.

The band came on and did their show, and Susan said it was terrific. But, after the band finished their encore song, and as they were leaving the stage, the drummer took his two wood drumsticks and threw them into the crowd. He didn't just toss them underhand into the crowd. He threw them overhand...hard.

The blunt end of one of the drumsticks hit Susan right between her green eyes, right above her eyebrows.

She fell down to her seat immediately. Don simply thought that she sat down, and in the darkness and noise, could not see her face or hear her scream. She stood up again, and her face was covered with blood. Susan told Don that a drumstick had hit her face. Don grabbed her and sat her down, and began screaming for security personnel. Within seconds, two security personnel were present, and radioed for the paramedics standing by to come to her aid. The paramedics stopped the bleeding and bandaged her wound.

During this, Don picked up the drumstick from the floor. He told the security guy that the drummer had thrown the stick. The security guy went backstage and told the Road Manager what had happened. The Road Manager was furious.

You see, this was not the first time this had happened in their concerts. On two other occasions, at other concert venues, the drummer had done the same thing, and injured other people. Fortunately for those people, the injuries were not as severe as Susan's injury.

The Road Manager had already warned the drummer that if it should ever happen again the drummer would be fired.

The Road Manager went to the band's bus and got the drummer, told him what he'd done, and brought him out to where Don and Susan were. The drummer apologized to Susan, sitting there with a bandaged forehead and blood-covered clothing. The drummer took the stick he'd thrown, took a Sharpie pen and signed the words "I'm Sorry," signed his name, and handed the stick back to Susan.

Don and Susan left the amphitheatre and drove home. Don wanted to take Susan to the emergency room that night, but Susan just wanted to go home. The next morning, her head was throbbing, and they went to the emergency room at their local hospital. Don called a friend who was a plastic surgeon, and he met them at the hospital.

Examination of Susan found a concussion, and a starburst-shaped wound on her forehead. The plastic surgeon said that it would take a lot of delicate surgery to repair the wound, and that he was certain there would be a small scar between her eyes.

My assignment in this claim was to take a recorded statement from Don and Susan in the office of their attorney. I did take the statement. Don showed me the drumstick that they kept in a sealed plastic bag. I took photos of the drumstick and Susan's forehead. I accumulated the medical bills and sent the whole package to the insurance company.

The insurance company's claims examiner was actually thinking of fighting this claim in court. However, I advised him that they could not possibly win a court fight in a small Georgia county against the wife of a seated county judge…especially when Susan had the drumstick with the drummer's confession written on it! I recommended that the insurance company negotiate with the claimant's attorney immediately. I recommended to him that he be prepared to offer Don and Susan an amount in the low six figures.

The insurance company did settle the case for a large amount of money.

That band also has a new drummer.

CHAPTER TWENTY NINE

BUSINESS CLAIMS

This will be a few short paragraphs to those of you who own a business. I am writing another book just for business claims.

Mr. or Ms. Business Owner - in most ways, handling your claims need the same attention to detail that I show in the pages of this book. So, please read the book in its entirety and adapt the strategies to your business loss.

READ YOUR POLICY. If you do not understand what your policy says, meet with your agent and get ALL the questions answered. Or, call me and I can help you on a consulting basis.

Keep meticulous records.

Seriously consider hiring a Public Adjuster to handle your claim. Your job is to keep your business running at a very crucial time. Many businesses close after a big loss because the loss was so disruptive they couldn't recover in time. PAs expedite claims and usually help you recover far more money than if you handle the claim yourself, or allow the insurance company to handle it. If you can't find a PA in your area, contact me at my website and I'll find one for you.

Take your own photos of all damages, no matter if they are to the building, your equipment, your vehicles, your employees.

Take it upon yourself to get the estimates and documents you need to prove your loss, and do it quickly.

Run EVERYTHING past your attorney before you agree to it or sign a form.

If you have a liability claim, the insurance company has a contractual obligation to provide you with legal representation under certain circumstances. But you should still get your own legal counsel to advise you.

This following statement will sound cynical, but it's true: Prepare your claim just as if you are going to have to file suit and go to trial. If you think this way, you'll take much more precaution than just letting the adjuster do everything. You may be assured that any good adjuster is already preparing his file with an eventual lawsuit in mind…even if it never happens.

That's how I investigate a claim, my friend.

CHAPTER THIRTY

THE CRISPY CRITTER

In my first three or four years as an adjuster, I did a lot of trucking claims. We adjusters in that office were ALWAYS on call, and many times in the middle of the night my pager (remember pagers?) would go off, and I'd have to quickly drive to the accident scene, somewhere in metro Atlanta.

Sometimes the accident would be a rollover, as a trucker unfamiliar with Atlanta highways would go into an on-ramp or off-ramp too fast, and lay his truck over on its side.

Sometimes the accident would involve the truck and another vehicle.

One night, or I should say early morning, about 4:30 am, my phone rang next to my bed. It was the claims office for the company's hotline number. She told me that there had been an accident involving one of our trucking company clients, and that another vehicle was involved. The driver in that other vehicle had been killed. The wreck had occurred about 75 miles south of Atlanta on I-75 southbound, at a certain mile marker.

I got dressed and headed south on I-75.

When I got there, it was about 7:00 am. The trucker was still parked in the emergency lane on the right of the highway. A State Highway Patrol car was also still there. A fire truck was still there with their hoses out. And, the car was still there with the driver still inside. A flatbed wrecker was just getting ready to load the car onto the flatbed.

What I found out from the State Trooper was that this driver of this Nissan 300Z lived in Macon, about 100 miles south of Atlanta. He had driven up to Atlanta the night before to frequent some of the nude bars there. (We like to call them the "shoe shows," 'cause I've heard that's usually the only thing the girls are wearing).

He got back in his car about 2:00 am, very drunk, headed south on I-75 toward home. At the accident scene, I-75 southbound is three lane blacktop, with an emergency lane on the far right of the roadway. Apparently, this driver got sleepy and decided to pull his car over in the emergency lane and take a nap. Unfortunately, he didn't quite make it all the way to the right. He stopped his car just over the crest of a hill, in the right hand active lane, shut off his lights and turned off the car. He reclined his seat and got ready to take that nap. It appears that he thought he was in the emergency lane.

Only seconds later, our trucker was coming about 75 mph down I-75 south, in the right hand active lane. He came over the crest of that hill, and there was the 300Z…lights off, parked and dark. He only had time to jerk the wheel left in an attempt to miss the car. His front wheels missed the car, but all the back right tandems rolled over the 300Z…right over the driver's side. The impact ruptured the gas tank of the car, and the metal-to-metal crash showered the car with sparks, igniting the fuel.

The trooper figured that the driver never knew what hit him. He was dead before he burned inside the car.

Miraculously, our truck driver was able to maintain control of the truck, and it did not flip over. He was able to drive the truck to his destination later that day.

So children…what lessons can we learn from this story?

1. Shoe shows can kill you.
2. Driving drunk can kill you.
3. Not being able to count to three (lanes) when you're driving drunk can kill you.

CHAPTER THIRTY ONE

SETTLING YOUR CLAIM

Here are a few things that have been talked about in other chapters, but still need to be reinforced here…just to make sure that you do them.

PROPERTY CLAIMS

Waiver of Lien

A Waiver if Lien form is a simple legal form. The company or individual who signs the form agrees that the payment they receive is payment in full, and they give up their right to claim a mechanic's lien on your assets for the amount of money listed in the form.

Mechanic's Liens are troublesome to say the least. They happen when a vendor or contractor does work and doesn't get paid for it. That vendor or contractor goes to court and slaps a lien on your property for the amount that the Court awards him. That ties up your title or deed, and you can't sell your property without paying the Mechanic's Lien first.

The Waiver of Lien prevents the vendor or contractor from filing a lien against your property.

It's customary for a contractor or subcontractor to sign one of these forms EVERY TIME THEY GET PAID. That means that if you had a contractor working or repairing your house for three months, he would need to sign at least three separate Waiver forms…one every month he got paid.

In property losses, you may have contractors or subcontractors that are performing repairs for you. Make SURE that you have ALL persons who will get paid for repairs sign a Waiver of Lien form BEFORE you sign the check. (or before the bank signs the check if you have a lender managing a repair escrow account.)

This should be a non-negotiable issue. Either the vendor signs the Waiver of Lien form, or he doesn't get paid. Period.

You'll find a simple Waiver of Lien form at the website in the Resources tab. Simply download a copy and fill in the blanks.

Sworn Statement in Proof of Loss

You'll find one of these forms at the website also. I'm going to call it a "Proof."

The Proof is only meant to settle the AMOUNT of a claim. It is NEVER used to settle whether certain damage is covered or not covered. Coverage questions are settled in a court of law. If your insurance company denies coverage on your damages, you may have to file suit to get a determination by a judge on coverage.

The Proof is a form signed by the Insured, between the Insured and the insurance company. This is a two party form only. The Proof is mentioned in your policy. Many insurance companies require this form to be signed before they release any money in settlement of a claim. Many times the insurance company will allow partial Proofs to be signed by the insured when they pay advances.

If you had a fire at home, you would likely have Dwelling loss as well as Contents losses. Your Contents loss might be ready to settle before the Dwelling loss is ready. In that case, the insurance company would likely accept a partial Proof in the amount of the Contents settlement so that you'd not have to wait for your money.

Some times, there is a dispute between the Insured and the insurance company on the amount of the settlement. In order to prevent or stop the insurance company from stalling or delaying payment of the claim indefinitely, the insured (THAT'S YOU!) can sign a Proof and send it to the insurance company. The Homeowners insurance policy usually gives the company 60 days to respond. Business insurance policies (CP 0010 form) only give the insurance company 30 days to respond.

Be very careful as you fill out the form. If you have a Public Adjuster, ask him to help you complete the form. If not, simply be careful yourself.

If you have a lienholder on your property, do not fail to disclose the name and address of the lienholder. The insurance company will then issue a payment with your name and the lienholder listed on the check.

Remember, you should not sign a form of ANY KIND without your attorney reviewing the form first.

You should ALWAYS send the signed Proof to the insurance company by certified mail, return receipt requested.

Once the insurance company receives the form, they have to do one of two things:

1. Accept the form and pay the claim.
2. Reject the form and tell you why.

Choice #2 is very serious. The insurance company is in danger of an Unfair Claims Practices violation and a fine from the Department of Insurance of your state. I'm not saying that rejection of a Proof is an automatic violation. I'm just saying that they'd better have a really good reason for the rejection.

Either way, you're moving the claim toward completion.

CASUALTY CLAIMS

These can be:

-Auto liability
-Homeowners liability
-Business liability

I could go on for hours and pages about the many ways that liability claims are settled. However, this is a book about claims strategies. I'm not going to include recent court cases and impress you with my claims knowledge. The best advice I can offer here in this book is:

1. If you are in a situation in which you MIGHT be liable for damages to someone, consult your attorney IMMEDIATELY. I realize that the insurance policy MIGHT cover this loss and the insurance company MIGHT have to provide a defense for you. But you need to protect yourself FIRST. Your attorney will be happy to work with an insurance defense attorney if and when one is appointed by the insurance company. But there are defense strategies that need to be discussed BEFORE the insurance company gets your claim.

2. Remember Chapter 23, in which I negotiated a settlement with the insurance company for damages to my Caddy? The settlement principles of "three times specials" are true as a rule. Don't forget to use it in your negotiations. Start high...negotiate down slowly.

3. The generally accepted method of completing a liability claim in which you are the Claimant is the other party's insurance company will ask you to sign a Release form. A Release form basically states

that you accept the conditions of the settlement and that you give up your right to pursue any further damages from the other party. NEVER, EVER sign a Release form of ANY TYPE without your attorney reviewing it FIRST. Once it's signed it's too late.

4. Usually, when you are the Defendant (the person liable) and the other guy is the Claimant (the person with damage) the insurance company will defend you and negotiate on your behalf. Your insurance company will get the Claimants to sign as restrictive a Release form as they will agree to sign.

I'll deal with some liability issues in my monthly newsletter. There are also archived articles at the website about liability.

* * * * * * * *

Settling the claim is the reward at the end of your hard work. You will learn a lot about human behavior, negotiation, law, insurance contracts, repair costs, and just people in general through this process of getting your claim paid. But, if you have followed the strategies in this book to the best of your abilities, you should be able to see the tangible evidence of your work when you receive the check from the insurance company. It should be hundreds or thousands of dollars more than you would have received without your good work.

Here's wishing all my best to you. I am so honored that you have purchased my book. Thank you! I hope we have a long and mutually profitable relationship.

If you have a story about how this book helped you, I'd love to hear that story. Please go to the website and leave me an email message. I'll cheer for you when I read it. With your permission, I might even publish YOUR story in the newsletter!!

APPENDIX

This book has been written to be a book of strategy, showing you how to take control of your claim and collect hundreds or thousands of dollars MORE than you would if you were not in control.

It is my greatest desire that you will use the strategies found in this book. I purposefully did not try to fill the back pages of the book with forms, shrunken down to fit the format size of this book.

All the forms you will need will be found in the Resource section on my website. All you have to do is click on the form you need, and you can print the form in Word format. The forms are FREE!!

The website address is:

www.insurance-claim-secrets.com

At the website, you will also find a place to sign up for my <u>FREE</u> monthly newsletter. That newsletter will give you terrific information not just about claims, but topics like:

- Top Ten biggest insurance ripoffs
- How to save money on auto insurance
- How to save money on homeowners insurance
- Super deals on 3-day and 4-day driveaway vacations
- How to save THOUSANDS on your taxes each year!

- How to buy life insurance and NOT GET RIPPED OFF!!
- Identity Theft!!
- How to manage deductibles
- How to fight traffic tickets and win most every time
- What about liability umbrella policies?
- Getting your Last Will and Testament written FREE!
- How to buy renter's insurance
- How to take a home inventory of your contents
- Flood insurance
- Secrets about business insurance policies
- Beware of body shop ripoffs
- How to find a great insurance agent
- Investing and the Rule of 72
- Financial Planners, not insurance agents
- Boat, Motorcycle, Snowmobile, ATV insurance
- And MUCH, MUCH MORE!!!

Plus, see the newest and freshest monthly information on handling your money and protecting your assets.

If you only get ONE great idea from my monthly newsletter, it could save you THOUSANDS!

There will also be links to other websites that will add SUPER VALUE to your life.

Remember, I will NEVER share my newsletter subscriber list with ANYONE. THERE IS NO COST…unsubscribe at any time. We'll LOVE having you as part of the family while you're with us, and miss you if you leave!

Get Help from your State Department of Insurance

There is no Federal Department of Insurance. Thankfully, the states each set their own regulations and statutes for insurance. Each state has its own Department of Insurance where consumers can go to obtain assistance dealing with problems they're having with insurance companies.

Many times in this book, I've recommended that if you do not get satisfaction from the insurance company or the claims adjuster in getting your claim paid, you should contact your state's Department of Insurance.

There's a SUPER helpful website developed by the National Association of Insurance Commissioners. At that site, there is a map of the US and its territories. Click on your state, and it takes you right to your state's Department of Insurance website.

The website address is:

http://www.naic.org/state_web_map.htm

A word of encouragement here. I know people have a need to be nice, and try and get along with everyone. That's really an admirable quality. It stops being so admirable when the insurance company claims examiner or the claims adjuster are refusing to help you collect all of the money you are entitled to collect.

When your adjuster or the claims examiner at the insurance company "drags their feet" or "digs in their heels" and will not compromise in the processing of your claim, it's time to call in the people that regulate them...if only to make sure that they are not violating a state law.

After all, your tax dollars are funding this very valuable state governmental unit. And, I've found that the state departments of insurance usually favor the consumer, not the insurance companies.

The Department of Insurance is there to help you solve problems in your claims process.

USE THEM!!!

For those of you that might not have access to the website, here is a list of all of the state Insurance Departments.

Department of Insurance for all US States and Territories

ALASKA
Alaska Division of Insurance
550 West 7th Avenue, Suite 1560
Anchorage, AL 99501-3567
907-269-7900
Fax 907-269-7910

ALABAMA
Alabama Department of Insurance
201 Monroe Street
Montgomery, AL 36104
334-269-3550
Fax 334-241-4192

ARKANSAS
Arkansas Department of Insurance
12000 West 3rd Street
Little Rock, AR 72201
501-371-2600
Fax 501-371-2629

AMERICAN SAMOA
Office of the Governor
American Samoa Government
Pago Pago, AS 96799
684-633-4116
Fax 684-633-2269

ARIZONA
Arizona Department of Insurance
2910 North 44th Street, Suite 220
Phoenix, AZ 85018
602-912-8400
Fax 602-912-8452

FLORIDA
Department of Financial Services
State Capitol, Plaza Level Eleven
Tallahassee, FL 32399
850-413-2806
Fax 850-413-2950

CALIFORNIA
California Department of Insurance
300 Capitol Mall, Suite 1700
Sacramento, CA 95814
916-492-3500
Fax 916-445-6552

COLORADO
Colorado Division of Insurance
1560 Broadway, Suite 850
Denver, CO 80202
303-894-7499
Fax 303-894-7455

CONNECTICUT
Connecticut Department of
Insurance
153 Market Street, 7th Floor
Hartford, CT 06103
860-297-3800
Fax 860-566-7410

DISTRICT OF COLUMBIA
Department of Insurance
801 First Street, NE, Suite 701
Washington, DC 20002
202-727-8000
Fax 202-535-1196

DELAWARE
Delaware Department of Insurance
Rodney Building
841 Silver Lake Blvd.
Dover, Delaware
302-739-4251
Fax 302-739-5280

IDAHO
Idaho Department of Insurance
700 West State Street, 3rd Floor
Boise, ID 83720
208-334-4250
Fax 208-334-4398

GEORGIA
Georgia Department of Insurance
2 Martin Luther King Jr. Drive
Floyd Building, 704 West Tower
Atlanta, GA 30334
404-656-2056
Fax 404-656-4688

GUAM
Department of Rev. & Taxation
Government of Guam
1240 Route 16
Barrigada, Guam 96913
671-635-1843
671-633-2643

HAWAII
Hawaii Insurance Division
Dep't. of Consumer Affairs
335 Merchant Street, Room 213
Honolulu, HI 96811
808-586-2790
Fax 808-586-2806

IOWA
Iowa Division of Insurance
330 E. Maple Street
Des Moines, IA 50319
515-281-5523
Fax 505-281-3059

LOUISIANA
Louisiana Department of Insurance

1702 N. 3rd Street
Baton Rouge, LA 70802
225-342-5423
Fax 225-342-8622

MASSACHUSETTS
Division of Insurance
Commonwealth of Massachusetts
One South Station, 5th Floor
Boston, MA 02110
617-521-7794
Fax 617-521-7758

ILLINOIS
Illinois Division of Insurance
320 West Washington St., 4th Floor
Springfield, IL 62767

217-785-5516
217-524-6500

INDIANA
Indiana Department of Insurance
311 W. Washington Street, Suite 300
Indianapolis, IN 46204

317-232-2385
Fax 317-232-5251

KANSAS
Kansas Department of Insurance
420 SW 9th Street
Topeka, KS 66612

785-296-3071
Fax 785-296-7805

KENTUCKY
Kentucky Office of Insurance
215 W. Main Street
Frankfort, KY 40601
502-564-6027
Fax 502-564-1453

MINNESOTA
Minnesota Department of
Commerce
85 7th Place East, Suite 500
St Paul, MN 55101
651-296-5769
Fax 651-282-2568

MISSOURI
Missouri Department of Insurance
301 West High Street, Suite 530
Jefferson City, MO 65101

573-751-4126
Fax 573-751-1165

MARYLAND
Maryland Insurance Administration
525 St. Paul Place
Baltimore, MD 21202
410-468-2090
410-468-2019

MAINE
Maine Bureau of Insurance
State Office Building, Station 34
Augusta, ME 04333
207-624-8401
Fax 207-624-8599

MICHIGAN
State of Michigan
Office of Financial & Insurance Services
611 W. Ottawa, 3rd Floor
Lansing, MI 48909
517-373-0220
Fax 517-373-4870

NORTH CAROLINA
North Carolina Department of Insurance
430 N. Salisbury Street
Raleigh, NC 27603
919-733-3058
Fax 919-733-6495

NORTH DAKOTA
North Dakota Department of Insurance
600 East Boulevard
Bismarck, ND 585505
701-328-2440
Fax 701-328-4880

NEBRASKA
Nebraska Department of Insurance
Terminal Building, Suite 400
941 "O" Street
Lincoln, NE 68508
402-471-2201
Fax 402-471-4610

NORTH MARIANA ISLANDS
Department of Insurance
Caller Box 10007 CK
Saipan, MP 96950
670-664-3000

MISSISSIPPI
Mississippi Insurance Department
501 North West Street
Jackson, MS 39205
601-359-3569
Fax 601-359-2474

MONTANA
Montana Department of Insurance
840 Helena Avenue
Helena, MT 59601

406-444-2040
406-444-3497

NEVADA
Nevada Division of Insurance
788 Fairview Drive, Suite 300
Carson City, NV 89701
775-687-4270
Fax 775-687-3937

NEW YORK
New York Department of Insurance
One Commerce Plaza, Suite 1700
Albany, NY 12257
518-474-4567
Fax 518-473-4139

OHIO
Ohio Department of Insurance
2100 Stella Court
Columbus, OH 43215

614-644-2658
Fax 614-644-3743

NEW HAMPSHIRE
New Hampshire Department of Insurance
21 South Fruit Street, Suite 14
Concord, NH 03301
603-271-2261
Fax 603-271-1406

NEW JERSEY
New Jersey Department of Insurance
20 West State Street, CN325
Trenton, NJ 08625
609-633-7667
Fax 609-984-5273

NEW MEXICO
New Mexico Department of Insurance
PERA Building, 1200 Pasa de Peralta
Santa Fe, NM 87504
505-827-4601
Fax 505-476-0326

PUERTO RICO
Puerto Rico Department of Insurance
1607 Ponce de Leon Avenue Stop 23
Santurce, Puerto Rico 00910
787-722-8686
Fax 787-722-4400

RHODE ISLAND
Rhode Island Insurance Division
233 Richmond Street, Suite 233
Providence , RI 02903
401-222-5466
Fax 401-222-5475

SOUTH CAROLINA
South Carolina Department of Insurance
300 Arbor Lake Drive, Suite 1200
Columbia, SC 29202
803-737-6227
Fax 803-737-6159

SOUTH DAKOTA
South Dakota Division of Insurance
445 East Capitaol Avenue, 1st Floor
Pierre, SD 57501
605-773-4104
Fax 605-773-5369

OKLAHOMA
Oklahoma Department of Insurance
2401 NW 23rd Street, Suite 28
Oklahoma City, OK 73107
405-521-2828
Fax 405-521-6635

OREGON
Oregon Insurance Division
350 Winter Street NE, Room 440
Salem, OR 97301
503-947-7980
Fax 503-378-4351

PENNSYLVANIA
Pennsylvania Insurance Department
1426 Strawberry Square, 13th Floor
Harrisburg, PA 17120
717-783-0442
Fax 717-772-1969

UTAH
Utah Department of Insurance
3110 State Office Building
Salt Lake City, UT 84114
801-538-3800
Fax 801-538-3829

VIRGINIA
Virginia Bureau of Insurance
1300 East Main Street
Richmond, VA 23219
804-371-9694
Fax 804-371-9873

VIRGIN ISLANDS
Division of Banking and Insurance
1131 King Street, Suite 101
Christiansted, St. Croix, VI 00802
340-773-6449
Fax 340-773-4052

VERMONT
Vermont Division of Insurance
89 Main Street, Drawer 20
Montpelier, VT 05620
802-828-3301
Fax 802-828-3306

TENNESSEE
Tennessee Department of Insurance
Davy Crockett Tower, 5th Floor
500 James Robertson Parkway
Nashville, TN 37243
615-741-6007
Fax 615-532-6934

TEXAS
Texas Department of Insurance
333 Guadalupe Street
Austin, TX 78701
512-463-6464
Fax 512-475-2005

WEST VIRGINIA
West Virginia Insurance Commission
1124 Smith Street
Charleston, WV 25301
304-558-3354
Fax 304-558-0412

WASHINGTON
Washington Dept. of Insurance
5000 Capitol Way
Tumwater, WA 98501

360-725-7000
Fax 360-586-3109

WISCONSIN
Wisconsin Department of Insurance
125 South Webster, GEF III, 2nd Fl.
Madison, WI 53702
608-267-1233
Fax 608-261-8579

WYOMING
Wyoming Department of Insurance
Herschler Building
122 W. 25th Street, 3rd East
Cheyenne, WY 82002
307-777-7401
Fax 307-777-5895

Made in the USA
Lexington, KY
11 November 2011